LIGHTING UP THE DARK-TUNNEL MOMENTS

A COMPREHENSIVE PASTORAL STUDY GUIDE

HARTNESS SAMUSHONGA

WESTBOW
PRESS®
A DIVISION OF THOMAS NELSON
& ZONDERVAN

www.lightingupthedark-tunnelmoments.com

WestBow Press books may be ordered through booksellers or by contacting:

WestBow Press
A Division of Thomas Nelson & Zondervan
1663 Liberty Drive
Bloomington, IN 47403
www.westbowpress.com
1 (866) 928-1240

ISBN: 978-1-9736-1718-1 (sc)
ISBN: 978-1-9736-1720-4 (hc)
ISBN: 978-1-9736-1719-8 (e)

Library of Congress Control Number: 2018901071

Print information available on the last page.

WestBow Press rev. date: 03/21/2018

CONTENTS

ACKNOWLEDGMENTS

I thank my Lord and Savior Jesus Christ for calling, equipping and commissioning me to be Pastor, so that I can lead, guide and support His people to be built-up and mature in faith and Godly-knowledge (Ephesians 4:11). I am also grateful to the Holy Spirit for the inspiration and strength to write this book in order to extend His ministry in me beyond borders.

I also appreciate my wife, my friend and supporter, Fungai. Her steadfast support for this project is overwhelming. Thank you to my children Enoch and Alicia for sacrificing our time together. Thank you for understanding what it meant each time I said, "I am sorry but I am very busy at the moment." Your patience has enabled the completion of this project with less challenge. I love you all dearly.

PREFACE

Everyone in this world will go through a difficult situation at some point in life. It is therefore common that Christians will sometimes find their faith shaken, hope shattered, and their relationship with Christ affected—when presented with challenges. Such circumstances will cause people to ask some deep questions about their situations, and how best to respond to them. These questions will include the following: (1) why do 'bad' things happen to Christians?, (2) How do I keep my faith alive when struggling with the issues of life?, (3) How can I pray more effectively—when things are not working well for me and (4) how should I behave when I feel like I am not receiving answers to my prayers? These are some of the questions I have also asked in my early Christian life, when I faced challenges. After I became involved in helping others more as a pastor, my eyes were open to how many people are asking the same questions. This motivated me to search for some answers to these complex questions. This involved some long-term in-depth study of scripture that incorporated prayer and reflecting on personal experiences and those of others.

There are no quick answers to most of life's challenges and questions. This book however provides a framework of how to think through situations, pray more effectively about difficult situations and how to remain connected with God—even in the most difficult of life-challenges. I offer an approach that is underpinned by biblical principles and the principles of Practical Theology—that can be applied in life situations of all kinds. After applying and practicing these principles in my life for many years—my life has never been the same since! I have consequently shared, taught and explored these insights with other Christians, in a variety of life and Christian ministry settings. I constantly see and hear life-stories of how these insights have enabled people to: (1) better understand their situations, (2) effectively pray over them and receive positive results and (3) maintain peaceful and fulfilled lives, even in the face of trying times. I have followed the encouragement of some of the people I have supported, and the prompting of the Holy Spirit—to make these insights available to a wider audience—well beyond the confines of my physical boundaries. I am therefore excited to share the wisdom in this book—which will also include some of my personal experiences and that of (unnamed) others.

Lighting up the dark-tunnel moments takes a practical and theologically balanced approach. It offers insights and approaches that are not only theoretical, but those that have been successfully applied by other believers, to navigate through undesirable and challenging life-moments. It takes the reader on a journey of exploring some theological themes and issues—that are associated with the experiences of difficulties. It employs a basic form of *theological reflection* (explained in more detail in chapter 6). Each chapter of the book covers a specific theme in great depth. The chapters of the book can be read and studied individually. However, the book is uniquely organised in such a way that each chapter builds towards the next. This gives the reader more tools and a robust framework for responding to difficult situations more effectively, with a better understanding and application of the Bible. I am hopeful that *Lighting up the dark-tunnel moments* provides an encouraging guidebook to help believers find light in the darkness and turn to God for guidance and purpose. This guidebook is useful for the individual Christian as well as pastors and Bible teachers—who have the important responsibility of supporting those who are going through the inevitable experience, of facing life-difficulties as a Christian.

In summary, it is my hope that through this book the reader will:

1. Have a general understanding of why things go wrong in the present world.
2. Be more aware of and have the understanding of the core factors (natural, human and spiritual) that influence difficult situations to occur—and how to respond to them.
3. Learn some forms of intense prayer that are relevant for responding to life difficulties.
4. Experience Holy Spirit inspired joy and peace of mind through times of difficulty.
5. Be equipped to impart these principles and insights to others.

CHAPTER 1

Introduction

Psalm 119:105 (NIV) reads, "Your word is a lamp to my feet and a light for my path." From this passage we can draw three ways in which we can understand life: (1) life as a journey, (2) the journey may involve travelling through the dark, and (3) that the Word of God is a source of light that shines through the dark. By understanding life as journey, this scripture gives the reassurance that the Word of God is a lamp to our feet and a light for our path in the journey of life. The consideration of life and more specifically, the Christian life—as a journey is widely accepted. This may stem from the fact that a journey is more or less universally understood as having a starting point, followed by a course (progression or journeying stage) and finally an end or arrival point (destination). From this perspective, we can consider that life in its earthly form has a timeline that is marked with a beginning and an end point (Genesis 3:19; Ecclesiastes 3:20; Job 14:1–2; 1 Corinthians 15:50). The progression phase between the beginning of life and the end mirrors the concept of journeying. Life is therefore not idle. Rather it is dynamic and progresses with the passing of time. Therefore, as time passes, experiences unfold along the journey.

While journeys can be enjoyable, it is not unusual for them to be marked with various activities and experiences that may include undesired setbacks. These will vary, and they may include bad weather, road maintenance, vehicle breakdown etc. These can lead to travel delays. Likewise, while life can be enjoyable, it is common to encounter undesired experiences in the course of both our life and Christian journeys. In light of Psalm 119:105, the negative phases of life are reflective of the moments we journey through the *dark-tunnel* experiences. We therefore need some support to navigate our way through life and the Christian journey itself. This Psalm reminds and encourages believers that when all forms of help and support fail, The Lord, through His Word, will support and sustain us through situations. In the analogy of Psalm 119:105, the Lord plays the role of: (1) a lamp that provides light to show us where we actually are in terms of the situations we face—as depicted by a lamp unto our feet and (2) where we need to go—as depicted by the light in our path (route of life). According to Adam Clarke's commentary on this verse, "God's word is a candle which may be held in the hand to give us light in every dark place and chamber."[1]

---

[1] Adam Clarke, "Commentary on Psalm 119:105" in *The Adam Clarke Commentary* (1832), accessed July 6, 2017, http://www.studylight.org/commentaries/acc/view.cgi?bk=ps&ch=119.

CHAPTER 2

Facing the Harsh Reality of Life

Our experience of life on earth as humans presents an ongoing paradox. Some moments or phases of life are enjoyable, and yet others are thorny and undesirable. The term *life* can be associated with either negative or positive experiences. Others have described the experience of a positive or high-quality life as "living the life." On the other hand, the term "that's life" has been used when coming to terms with the negativities of life. Most people would have experienced both sides of life described by these phrases—even without necessarily using these phrases. Life is thus very precious, but also very vulnerable. There are various factors that influence the experiences of challenges in our lives. From the beginning of time, people everywhere in the world have, and still continue to encounter situations that threaten their experience of blissful life and the pursuit of happiness. This is a universal experience of human life. Everyone will at some point in their lives encounter experiences that affect their comfort, peace of mind, stability and security. They are so many to mention, and will include but are not limited to loneliness, bereavement, victimization and abuse, ill-health or poor well-being, disability, parenting a child with challenging behavior or personality, looking after a beloved one with special needs, fertility or conception challenges, family/relationship tensions, spiritual challenges, ministry struggles, business challenges, challenging employment situations etc. Such experiences undoubtedly have the potential to affect the enjoyment of life that we so desire. While we may not be able to prevent or eliminate all of these challenges, as believers, we have comfort in knowing that God's Word revealed in the Bible can guide us in overcoming such situations and to endure challenges in a more positive way.

Faith Is Vulnerable in Times of Difficulty

The connection between our state of mind, faith and prayer is vital. Some important inferences from the Bible can help us to understand this link. The Bible says "Love the Lord your God with all your **heart** and with all your **soul** and with all your **mind**" (Matthew 22:37 NIV). This verse shows that the mind is connected to the practice and experience of worship. Therefore, when the mind is affected, there is the risk that our worship and relationship with God is also affected. For instance, if someone is gripped by anxiety or fear arising from a bad experience, his or her faith (the belief that God can positively intervene in the situation) may be shaken. Under such circumstances, one can easily overlook God's omnipotence (that God has the ability to do anything, including intervening in the situation). It is common for people to find it more difficult to pray and seek God's intervention in their situations (as encouraged in Philippians 4:6 –7)—when overwhelmed by situations. This could lead to becoming withdrawn from Christian practices and activities such as prayer, reading the Bible and fellowship (engaging with other believers for collective worship or for peer support and encouragement). Others have found themselves on the verge of turning their backs on their faith—in the absence of support and encouragement from others. Thankfully, the teaching and practice of Christian faith presented in the Bible involves collective worship and carrying each other's burdens (Galatians 6:2). Christianity involves and allows for others (including fellow Christians and or ministers) to support and offer prayers for those who find themselves in such situations (Acts 12:5; Ephesians 6: 18; James 5:14 –16). This is one supportive mechanism that is very effective in supporting those enduring difficult situations that is usually not fully utilized—by both the individuals experiencing the situations and those around them—who may be well positioned to support them.

It is true that the contemporary world has influenced (secularized) religious and Christian practices.[2] This is largely as a result of the changes in culture. It is widely acknowledged that the 21st century mindset has increasingly become individualistic. While some of the characteristics and principles of individualism such as independence and the emphasis on personal worth and achievements are positive aspects of life[3], an extreme embrace of individualistic culture that disregards biblical principles of collectivism can be detrimental. As an example, this approach may cause Christians to endure challenging times without social or prayer support. It has been my observation that contemporary church programs have become more and more designed in ways that allow little opportunity to pray over those experiencing challenging situations of life. There is a place for both individual prayers and a place to have others support and pray for us. The Bible clearly encourages the body of believers to support each other in prayer and highlights that within the body of believers; there are those with specific Spiritual Gifts (God given supernatural abilities) to positively impact the wellbeing of the people of God in various aspects of life, as shown in 1 Corinthians.

---

[2] Alan Aldridge, *Religion in the Contemporary World: A Sociological Introduction* (Cambridge: Polity Press, 2000).

[3] Dan J. Rothwell, *In the Company of Others: An Introduction to Communication* (New York: Oxford University Pres, 2010), 65–84.

CHAPTER 3

Correcting the Fantasy of a Problem-free Life

We are fortunate to live in the age of better access to information. Today's Christian has access to a limitless resource of inspiring Christian resources and material. This will come in the form of books and audio and video resources. Like in many disciplines, media has been effectively used to broadcast Christian material on various themes or topics in order to inspire believers. This include three philosophies that I would like to briefly discuss here, which are relevant to the theme of this book, namely: (1) *Positive confession*, which generally teaches that words and thoughts of a believer are powerful, and that thinking and speaking out positive statements from the Bible will determine your future and destiny, (2) *The gospel of health*, which in its extreme form generally teaches that every believer should live healthy lives and should never become unwell and (3) *The gospel of wealth* (or prosperity gospel), which in its extreme form generally teaches that it is God's plan for every Christian to be wealthy, and that financial lack, need or poverty is a sign of living outside of God's will and principles. Some believers have found these teachings uplifting and beneficial—particularly as a means of inspiring hope in the face of difficulties. Others have on the other hand, understandably, found these philosophies confusing—especially after challenging situations such as ill-health and financial lack; even after following the principles of positive confession described above. Sadly, others have been left in a place where they start to question their faith altogether. This chapter will discuss this issue in more depth in order to set a strong biblical basis that is necessary in providing a better interpretation of situations. This will in turn equip Christians to respond to life challenges more positively.

I wish to highlight that the positive confession and the gospels of health and wealth do have some biblical basis because: (1) it is desirable and beneficial for believers to meditate on *(and confess)* the Word of God (Joshua 1:8) (Psalms 1:1–3), (2) believers should trust and believe God for good health (Isaiah 50:4) and (3) believers should trust and believe God for financial blessing or stability (Deuteronomy 8:18). In fact, 3 John 1:2 NASB aptly summarizes this: "Beloved, I pray that in all respects you may prosper and be in good health, just as your soul prospers". We can see here that the Bible instills the view that believers should trust and expect God to bless (prosper) them in all areas of life, including health. Also, scripture teaches that exercising faith (James 1:6) and dealing with sin (Isaiah 59:1–2) enhances our relationship with God, and our experiences of God's blessings. However, while the Bible teaches us to trust and believe God for enhancement of life, including the aspects of health and finances, it should be emphasized that an unbalanced presentation of positive confession messages and the gospels of health and wealth deviates from the message of the Bible. The teaching that Christians should expect to consistently and eternally enjoy trouble-free lives is very problematic, and not consistent with the teaching of the Bible. If that were the case, we really would not need the Bible in its present form—as a significant part of the Bible is aimed at inspiring and guiding believers on how to overcome or endure trials, temptation and life challenges—when, rather than if, they present.

People have been led to believe that by merely confessing health and wealth, they will constantly live healthy and wealthy. This is however not how it works in reality. This is also not what the Bible says. Some of those who have followed such teachings have been disappointed and confused—when their confessions did not yield results. There has also been situations where labels have been attached to believers found to experience such challenges as ill health or financial instability. Believers have been labeled as, or made to feel that: (1) they have lack of faith, (2) they do not fully apply the principle of positive confession in their lives, (3) they are more sinful than others or (4) they are distant from God. We however see in reality that people (including believers) who are not careful with their diet and do not exercise adequately—are more prone to some medical conditions. Similarly, life and scripture demonstrates that those (including believers) who have opportunities to work but choose to be idle, are more prone to lack and need. On this, the Bible says that "All hard work brings a profit, but mere talk leads only to poverty" (Proverbs 14:23 NIV). In other words, an idle believer who does not maximize the opportunities that God offers them is more likely to be in need or more at risk of poverty—no matter how much they merely confess prosperity. This is what has been described as "dead faith"—faith not backed by action (James 2:14 –26). There are indeed situations where faith will require corresponding action; beyond just speaking or confessing positively.

I am of course not implying that everyone who is unwell or of ill-health does not eat healthy or exercise. Neither am I suggesting that everyone who is in need or affected by poverty is lazy, No! I am well aware that ill-health may arise as a result of other factors that are beyond the control of an individual—such as genetics, supernatural factors and other unknown factors. I equally acknowledge that there are other situations that cause need, lack or poverty that people do not have control over. Examples include but are not limited: to family background or circumstances, lack of or limited opportunities, natural disasters etc. The purpose of highlighting the unbalanced views of positive confession and the 'gospels of health' and 'gospel of wealth' (prosperity) is not simply to criticize these views. That is not my objective—as I have already acknowledged that, these views have some biblical basis. It is however misleading and unbiblical to strongly advocate: (1) that believers should live perfect lives that are free from challenge and (2) that going through a difficult situation is a reflection of lack of faith, sinful nature or being distant from God. I now turn attention to scriptures to illustrate this point further.

No One is Immune to Life Challenges

The life of one great apostle and teacher of the gospel of *salvation through faith in Jesus*, Paul, effectively addresses this issue. He declared, "I know what it is to be in need, and I know what it is to have plenty. I have learned the secret of being content in any and every situation, whether well fed or hungry, whether living in plenty or in want" (Philippians 4:12 NIV). Apostle Paul after becoming a follower of Jesus Christ (Acts 9) lived a life of total dedication to God. He is a good example of someone who was *sold-out* for God and His purposes. For instance, even after he was prophetically warned of impending imprisonment if he were to go to Jerusalem, he pronounced that he was "ready not only to be jailed at Jerusalem but even to die for the sake of the Lord Jesus" (Act 21:13 NLT). Even with this deep devotion to his faith, his life was marred with experiences of hardship. Acts 16:19 – 40 describes some of the undesirable experiences he went through, together with one of his companions Silas, which included: (1) being spitefully and falsely accused of treason (vs21), (2) being attacked by a mob, (3) being stripped of their clothes in public, (4) being severely physically assaulted (vs23) and (5) thereafter, being imprisoned under harsh and more restricting conditions (vs23 – 24).

Furthermore, in his encouragement to the believers in Corinth, in 2 Corinthians 6:3 –10 (NLT), Paul elaborates on some of the difficulties he endured:

We live in such a way that no one will stumble because of us, and no one will find fault with our ministry. In everything we do, we show that we are true ministers of God. We patiently endure **troubles** and **hardships and calamities of every kind**. We **have been beaten**, been **put in prison**, **faced angry mobs**, worked to exhaustion, endured **sleepless nights**, and **gone without food**. We prove ourselves by our purity, our understanding, our patience, our kindness, by the Holy Spirit within us,[a] and by our sincere love. We faithfully preach the truth. God's power is working in us. We use the weapons of righteousness in the right hand for attack and the left hand for defense. We serve God whether people honor us or despise us, whether they slander us or praise us. We are honest, but **they call us impostors**. We are **ignored**, even though we are well known. **We live close to death**, but we are still alive. We have been beaten, but we have not been killed. Our **hearts ache**, but we always have joy. **We are poor**, but we give spiritual riches to others. **We own nothing**, and yet we have everything [Emphasis added].

Paul in this passage primarily highlights the supernatural relief and comfort that God provided for him in the face of difficulties—some of which he lists in the passage. We therefore learn from Paul's experiences that: (1) like Paul, believers do encounter difficulties of various forms and (2) going through challenges is not necessarily associated with lack of faith—as sometimes presented in the unbalanced views of positive confession and 'gospels' of health and prosperity. It is clear from the Bible that Paul extensively taught on faith, and that he exercised faith in his own life. While we acknowledge that Paul was a man of faith, there are times that he encountered difficulties. It should therefore be expected that believers—including those that are firm in their faith will face challenges. There is however the hope that the Lord is our source of strength and solutions through the Holy Spirit.

Like Paul, the Bible presents Job as another example that demonstrates that those that follow God's principles are not immune to the experience of difficulties. Job is presented as one whom God Himself affirmed to be righteous. We however learn that his journey of life was too characterized by a season of great difficulties. This is in spite of the Lord Himself testifying of Job's character: "He is the finest man in all the earth. He is blameless—a man of complete integrity. He fears God and stays away from evil" (1:8 NLT). Clearly, from God's own perspective, Job's life was modeled on God's principles. Nevertheless, we see a consistent message, as with the example of Apostle Paul, that in spite of this character that is devoted to God, Job went through some time of difficulty: (1) all his livestock (source of wealth) and all his children died on the same day (1:13 –22) and (2) his body was physically covered with lesions—which are often understood as boils or ulcers (2:7). It should be understood here that although we can read the entire book of Job in a matter of minutes or hours, Job's ordeal spanned years. Likewise, there will be some difficult situations that will last for a long time in our lives. Nonetheless, the Bible does not attribute Job's difficulties to sin, lack of faith or any failure on his part. The opposite is actually true. Job was totally committed to God and to His principles. The text shows that God Himself was pleased with the way Job lived his life, as highlighted above.

From Paul and Job's accounts, we can conclude that experiencing difficult situations is part and parcel of life on earth (fallen world). It is to be expected. More importantly, we should not consider such experiences to be signs of sinfulness or lack of faith. These two examples demonstrate that those who exercise faith (like Paul) or lead lives that are pleasing to God (like Job) will, too, face life-challenges and difficulties. In presenting this *truth*, I am not 'preaching' a *message of misery*: i.e. that believers should live miserable lives, NO! I consider life a precious gift from God that is endowed with wonderful pleasures that He intends for us to enjoy. And most people do enjoy life in many instances. Thanks be to God. We however stray from the truth if we expect the sinful world that carries the curse (that came as a result of disobedience) to be perfect. The present world is not a perfect world. The perfect World (widely known as heaven) is still to come. The Bible clearly shows that the perfect world will be ushered by the second coming (return) of our Lord Christ (see Philippians 3:20; 2 Thessalonians 1:6 – 7; 1 Peter 3:5). This is not to say that we should not expect to enjoy life in the present world. The Bible actually says: "there is nothing better for people than to be happy and to do good while they live" (Ecclesiastes 3:12 NIV). The scripture goes on to say that, "so I commend the enjoyment of life, because there is nothing better for a person under the sun than to eat and drink and be glad. Then joy will accompany them in their toil all the days of the life God has given them under the sun" (8:1 NIV). This means that there are many opportunities to enjoy life, even though we experience occasions and periods of challenges and difficulties. This is of course not referring to the enjoyment of life that is contrary to the teaching and principles of God's Word such as sexual immorality, wild parties, drunkenness etc. The Word of God clearly condemns such practices of enjoyment of life in Galatians 5:16 –21.

Therefore, as unfortunate as it is, we should expect things to go wrong in our earthly lives. To be more precise, whether we like it or not, we will face diverse life challenging situations—no matter how much we confess positively. Accordingly, whatever you or someone you know or care about may be going through today, is typical of the present world. The challenges and the temptations we face are universal. The Bible can never be clearer; "The temptations in your life are no different from what others experience..." (1 Corinthians 10:13 NLT). This means that everyone will have his or her share of challenges, and that it is hardly possible that one will go through something that has never been experienced. I know that many a time, it does not feel that way—particularly when going through the challenges.

Of the estimated 7 Billion individuals in the world, it is very likely that someone somewhere will be facing a similar challenge, or that someone somewhere would have already gone through any kind of challenge that you will ever go through in your lifetime. While this in itself may not give you the reassurance you may need for a pressing situation, it illuminates a more reassuring understanding— that whatever situation you will ever encounter will not surprise God. That is really reassuring. It should be our comfort, that 'Jesus knows all our struggles' as in the wonderful hymn: 'There is not a Friend' by Johnson Oatman Jr. (1856 –1926). Jesus does not merely know of our troubles. He is also able to guide and inspire us to find solutions and better ways of coping and enduring difficulties— through the Holy Spirit.

The purpose of this chapter is to show that life troubles are universal and befall everyone, including Christians. Christians should therefore not beat themselves up and consider such challenges as signs of lack of faith, or that they are not confessing the Word of God enough. There will be times when things go wrong in our lives—even when our faith is strong, and when we are living right with the Lord. The next chapter proceeds to discuss the root of the problems in the world.

CHAPTER 4

Living in a Messed-up World

In this chapter, I will highlight and discuss the root source of life-problems—as presented in scripture. While that alone will not provide solutions to problems, it will give a better understanding that the problems of this world are rooted in, and are effects of the 'fall of mankind.' This will provide the assurance that God can rescue His people from the effects of the fall. Therefore, while the world is subject to the effects of the fall, we should still hope in the Lord—who is always looking out to help us from the challenges of the world we live in.

The Fall of Mankind

What is widely referred to as the 'fall of mankind' in theological thinking known as the original act in which humans deviated from God's intended plan. The Bible clearly shows that the present world is a 'fallen' world because of sin. Genesis 3 verses 1–7 highlights how the first two humans (Adam and Eve) yielded to temptation, and disobeyed God. Their act of disobedience resulted in the fall from place of obedience, trust and close friendship with God, which He had determined for them.

In verses 8–21 we discover that human suffering, guilt, hardship, pain, sorrow and death all entered the realm of human experience as a result of sin. Finally, in verses 22–24 we find the first human couple (Adam and Eve) expelled from Eden and beginning a much less satisfying existence (Quinn, 2009).[4] [brackets added]

The fall therefore corrupted the entire natural world, including human nature. While we may consider the world to be functional at a human level, we also know that the world now exists in a diminished state of perfection—far from what was originally desired by God, before the fall. Using a contemporary analogy, it will be like having a corrupted computer program, which while functional—its functionality is far less optimized than the original (version). So, while the world is functional, and often we enjoy our lives, its systems and the lives of the people who inhabit it are far from perfect. By failing to uphold their part of the agreement with God, their Father and Creator, mankind opened themselves to some consequences. The key elements of the agreement are outlined in the Bible: "Then the LORD God took the man and put him into the Garden of Eden to cultivate it and keep it. The LORD God commanded the man, saying, 'From any tree of the garden you may eat freely. But from the tree of the knowledge of good and evil you shall not eat, for in the day that you eat from it you will surely die." (Genesis 2:15 –17 NASB). Dying in this case can be understood as spiritual death, physical death or both. Genesis 5:5 reveals that Adam eventually died physically.

---

[4] Quinn, Jon. W, "Direction for Living in a Fallen World" in The Expository Files, 2009, accessed February 21, 2017.
https://www.bible.ca/ef/topical-directions-for-living-in-a-fallen-world.htm.

Hope to Overcome

It is common for people to wonder God treated mankind harshly for their disobedience. The opposite is however true. While mankind deserve eternal condemnation and death, God made provision for their redemption: "For the sin of this one man Adam, caused death to rule over many. But even greater is God's wonderful grace and his gift of righteousness, for all who receive it will live in triumph over sin and death through this one man, Jesus Christ" (Romans 5:17 NLT). God made provision for mankind to avoid eternal death. He instead offered us eternal life through Christ. However, although God has redeemed the world from its fallen nature, the perfect plan of God will not be fulfilled in this life—but a new life with Christ. This chapter however aims to help the reader realize and accept that challenges and problems in this life are essentially rooted in the fall of mankind, and are universal. This gives us the opportunity to explore our situation from a more informed position.

CHAPTER 5

Breaking Down Situations

In the last chapter I discussed the root of the fallen state of the world. I highlighted the fact that deviating from God's plan exposes the world to all sorts of problems and challenges. Before we turn our attention to exploring some of the broad factors that cause undesirable life situations or experiences to occur, or how to respond to them, it is important to understand that situations are themselves unique and complex. It therefore demands that when reflecting on life-pressing situations, we should do so with depth, by breaking the situations down.

It is often easy to recognize difficult and challenging situations when they present in our lives. We usually recognize them by the symptoms (manifestations and experiences) of how they affect us. As an example, when one is feeling physically unwell, the symptoms may manifest in experiences of physical pain or some other physical debilitation. In the case of a relationship breakdown, the manifesting symptoms may include experiences of hurt (heartache) and feelings such as loneliness, rejection, betrayal etc. The symptoms however signal the presence of an underlying problem or challenge in an individual's life.

Situations are complex. Although we are usually able to identify that something is wrong in our lives, it is often not easy to take time to fully understand a situation, or attempt to identify the *source* of the problem (the real problem). It is likely that where there is tension in relationship, the tension itself can be seen as the problem. The real problem can however be an underlying factor such as lack of, or ineffective communication. It is true that the situation itself is a problem. However, another way of looking at it is to consider *the source of the situation* as 'the problem'—for without it, the situation would be different. From that perspective, we can see ineffective communication to be 'the problem' (the source of the situation). In other situations the 'real problem' could be how we chose to respond or how we cope with a difficult situation, rather than the situation itself. I experienced this when my dad passed away, as I will explain. At this point it will suffice to say that exploring a situation in line with the Word of God is vital, and is essential for identifying and addressing key problems in the life of a believer.

Reflecting On Situations

It is helpful to explore the nature of situations from a Practical Theological perspective. Let me begin by giving a simplified definition of Practical Theology. Practical Theology is concerned with looking at situations of human experience, and reflecting on them critically, from various perspectives. This is aimed at understanding the situation in more depth, and figuring out how to appropriately apply God's Word in that and other related situations.[5] In one of the most valuable books I read in my study of Practical Theology, the authors highlight an important fact that "situations are complex multifaceted entities which need to be examined with care, rigor and discernment if they are to be effectively understood."[6] It is important that we understand

---

[5] Mowat, John and Harriet Swinton. *Practical Theology and Qualitative Research*. London: SCM, 2006.

[6] Mowat, John and Harriet Swinton. *"Practical Theology and Qualitative Research"* London: SCM, 2006.15.

a situation more deeply, before seeking ways to address the situation. A careful and intentional reflection on a situation will enable a more in-depth understanding of the situation. Often times, situations are more complicated than they appear at face value. However, we can understand a bit more about some of the situations we face if we took time to understand what the situation or problem really is. We however usually react and respond to situations before taking time to explore the situations in light of scripture. While we may not be able to reflect on each and every bad situation we encounter—it is possible to give more attention to those long lasting situations or those that affect us more severely. Taking time to explore these situations should however be an intentional exercise.

This will help in two ways. First, energy and efforts will be directed at seeking to address the actual problem, and not merely the symptoms. Secondly, it gives the opportunity to direct prayers towards the real problem or source of the situation. This approach is known as complexifying a situation. It refers to the critical reflection on a situation, at various levels, in order to gain more in-depth understanding of the situation.[7]

We should reflect on our situations in light of scripture through *theological reflection*. I have dedicated the whole of chapter 6 on theological reflection. Nevertheless, I will at this point, share a personal experience of *theological reflection* I went through, following my father's death. At the time, I did not know about theological reflection. It is through looking back at (reflecting on) the situation that I now understand that I had put theological reflection into practice. I have since adopted the principle of prayerfully reflecting on situations, and that always helps me when dealing with or enduring life-pressing challenges of various sorts.

---

[7] Mowat, John and Harriet Swinton. *"Practical Theology and Qualitative Research."*

My Personal Journey of Bereavement

Friday 19th November 1993 presented me with the most unexpected and most painful situation I had ever experienced. My parents had just returned home from their farm, which was some 80 miles out of town. They had spent the past few days there. After having dinner as a family, my mother had an acute asthma attack, collapsed, and went to be with the Lord. I was 17 at the time. This was not expected, at least from my perspective. Mum was known to have chronic asthma for years. She would have occasional episodes of exacerbation, but her asthma was generally well managed with inhalers and occasional steroidal tablets. Her passing on was really unexpected, as she was generally fit and healthy. The subsequent experience of not having a mother in the home significantly changed our home situation. Though my mother was actively engaged in some small scale merchandising business activities, as well as some small scale farming with dad, she was largely a housewife. She therefore spent more time at home. As a result, I generally spent more time with her outside of school time. Although dad had retired a few years before mum passed away, he served as a lay ministry leader in the local church. His ministry was however beyond our locality. I therefore spent more time with mum—being what my siblings jokingly described as the "spoilt last born child". This was probably true. As the last-born child, I think I was long-term breastfed—beyond the age of two. Nevertheless, as a teenager in the home, we used to have the typical mother-son fights regularly, and this kept my relationship with my mum real and close.

However, the years following mum's passing on saw a further strengthening of the bond of my relationship with dad. I was raised in a loving and caring home, and was always very close to both my parents. I however had a stronger bond with mum since I spent more time with her than dad, who as highlighted above, had a regular job. Even after his retirement, dad had some ministry engagements locally and beyond. Mum's death obviously affected us—as a family.

However, the sudden loss of my mother left my then retired, 63-year-old dad, very lonely. Mum and dad were so close. While we were all affected by mum's departure, it was evident that my dad was most affected by the loss of his dear wife. This deeply troubled me. I consequently resolved and pledged myself to always be there for him in all ways possible. I began to spend more time with dad. Much of my free time was spent driving him around—including for ministry trips. Instead of always going out with friends, I would sometimes bring my friends home, and we would all spend time with dad. Dad had an amazing personality. Most of my friends became friends with dad. The time I spent close to him was crucial. I leant much about Christianity, ministry and other key life principles in this time. Dad and I became so close that we would freely discus about who I was dating and the like.

However, on Friday October 10th 1998, after waving goodbye to my sister Barbara (who had visited home—as she lived in the same town with her family) and my niece Chipo, dad collapsed on the floor and became unconscious. He was immediately rushed to the hospital. I wasn't home at the time of the incident, so Barbara contacted me on my cell phone and informed me that dad had collapsed, and they had called an ambulance. I quickly drove home—as I was only a few minutes away. Barbara also called two leaders in our church who lived locally, and were close to dad—Deacons Simon and Emmanuel. I arrived home as he was being taken to hospital, and Deacon Simon was with him. Dad was unfortunately pronounced dead on arrival at the hospital.

I asked to see him. After being directed to the room where he was, I went up to him, and gave him a big long hug—kissed him and cried for a minute or two. After some time, I left the hospital accompanied by Deacon Emmanuel who had also come to the hospital. While walking to his car, I felt as if the whole world was silent, and that I was all alone in it. I went through a similar feeling I had experienced 5 years earlier, when mum passed away. This time it was worse. Probably because I was now a bit more mature in age, and understood more about what it meant to lose a parent. Also, my only parent had gone. Dad had chronic hypertension for many years, but he was generally well. Although he had been unwell in the preceding few weeks, his death was unexpected. It therefore came as a shock to me. I remember leaving the hospital and walking with Deacon Emmanuel to his car car—with both of us in total silence. He did not say anything much, apart from expressing his deepest sympathy, repeatedly. I'm glad he did not say much. I just wanted some quiet time. I suppose he too was in shock, and affected. He was quite close to my dad and my family. He was, in fact, one of the younger leaders whom my dad had mentored and supported in ministry. That is why my sister had rung both him and Deacon Simon to inform them that dad had collapsed at home.

While in the car on our way back home, I remember that my mind was processing thoughts at a very slow pace—trying to figure the next step. Firstly, just coming to terms with the fact that my father was dead consumed my mind. Secondly, I was also bracing myself to break the news to my sister Barbara and my niece Chipo—who had both witnessed dad collapse. They had remained home praying and hoping that he would recover. I only had a few minutes to prepare myself, as the drive from the hospital back to the house was about half an hour. I knew very well that Barbara was more fragile, and I was dreading having to break the news to her. I was also thinking about the other siblings living in various locations, who were still to be informed of dad's passing. These thoughts consumed my mind on the short drive home.

In the following few hours, every family member was eventually informed and they all rushed home as soon as they could to mourn together, support each other, and to make arrangements for the funeral. I thank God, that while the whole family was shocked and saddened by the loss of our so loved father, every one of us handled the loss better than I feared. Dad's funeral arrangements moreover went well with exceptional support from relatives and friends. Hundreds of people collectively—family, friends, the local community, our local church and many other ministry leaders from around the country—attended the funeral. This helped the situation in a similar way as with the support received following mum's death. However, after all the people had dispersed, the sense of loneliness crept in.

Having been the last child in the family, I was the only one of my siblings living at home at the time dad passed away. After dad's funeral, the rest of the family returned to their respective homes. The reality of the loss started to sink in. Now with my brothers and sisters having returned to their homes and families, I started to miss dad a great deal. We had become very close, as we would spend a lot of time together since mum passed away. As the days went by, it dawned to me that dad had really gone, and that I could not reverse it. From a Christian perspective, I can say that I was to a degree mature in my understanding of death. I think I had a fair understanding of the Bible view of death—particularly death of a believer. I never at any point questioned God on why my father had passed away. All the same, it was really distressing each time I thought about dad. I remember hoping that one way or the other, the Lord would comfort and strengthen me through His Spirit. I was also fully aware that at some point I would need to move on. I however knew I could not easily manage on my own, but that I needed God's help to enable me to move on.

Looking back and on the situation, I reflected on my emotional experiences at the time, in view of Kübler-Ross and Kessler's five phase model of grief, [8] which can be understood "as five *common* experiences—not five *required* experiences"[9] (Megan Devine, Huffington Post, As of August 30, 2017). It means not everyone will experience all five experiences in bereavement. These are denial, anger, bargaining, depression and acceptance. I will take time to

---

[8] Kübler-Ross, Elisabeth, and David Kessler. *On Grief and Grieving: Finding the Meaning of Grief Through the Five Stages of Loss.* New York: Scriber, 2005.
[9] Devine, Megan. "Stages of Grief." Accessed August 30, 2017. http://www.huffingtonpost.com/megan-devine/stages-of-grief_b_4414077.html.

explain my understanding of each one of Kübler-Ross and Kessler's five phase experiences below—as this may be helpful to someone:

1. *Experiencing denial* – This refers to the feeling where the individual is in some state of shock, and considers that the situation (e.g. death of a loved one) has not really happened. It may include the thought and feeling that there may be a mistake somewhere, and that the situation may not have actually happened. It may include the thought that the reality may be a dream, and the individual holds on to an opposite, or preferred reality.

2. *Experiencing anger* – This refers to the feeling where the individual does not or is no longer able to continue denying the reality of the situation—and becomes angry about the situation. This anger can be directed to others or self. This may manifest in the form of feelings, which may be associated with the asking of questions such as; "Why me? It's not fair!"; "How can this happen to me?"; "Who is to blame?"; "Why would this happen?"; "Why now?"

3. *Experience of bargaining* – This applies where there is the hope that the cause of grief can be reversed. It is characterized by the hope that the individual can avoid a cause of grief. This may include the thought of wanting to change, give up or sacrifice something, in order to reverse the situation. This may manifest in feelings such as; "I'd give anything to have him/her back." Or: "If only he'd come back to life, I'd promise to be a better person!"

4. *Experiences of being depressed* – The individual experiences despair as a result of the situation. They may become withdrawn, and spend much of the time mournful and sullen. They will go through feelings such as; "I'm so sad, why bother with anything?"; "I miss my loved one, why go on?" There is a sense or feeling of losing hope or motivation to move on.

5. *Acceptance* – The individual comes to accept the reality of the situation, and feels more able to face the new reality—in a more emotionally calm and stable way.

While these common experiences are not there to "dictate whether you are doing your grief "correctly" or not,"[10]—I found this a useful basis for reflecting on, and understanding my feelings in my experience of bereavement. However, I do not consider that I experienced all the five experiences. I remember experiencing three of these experiences: (1) *Denial*—Dad's death came as a shock. I had not seen it coming. I was in fact in denial for a few days. It was not easy to actually think it had happened. A part of me thought they may have made an error in clinically verifying his death, and hoped he would just wake up. Another part of me thought that if he had really died, God would bring him back to life, (2) *Anger*—I did feel angry. Even when I was no longer in denial, I felt that at 68, dad had died early. There was no real warning or preparation. I was nonetheless not angry with or at anyone; not God, not dad and not myself. I was angry at the situation. I was angry and asking, "why did it have to happen now?" and (3) *Acceptance*—Fortunately for me, it did not take a very long time to eventually accept the reality. I accepted that I needed to move on. I felt more able to face the new reality in a more emotionally calm and stable way. Of course it was painful, and it altered my life plans in significant ways.

I did not just come to accept this new reality. It was a process. I had to consciously consider some facts about the situation, in light of scripture. Dad had always been independent in regards to managing his health, finances and social life in general. Nonetheless, after mum passed away, I naturally assumed the role of ensuring dad was well—since I lived with him. In a way, that had become one of my preoccupations, which I enjoyed. Now it was suddenly not there. This created a void. On the other hand, there was a sense of

---

[10] Megan, "Stages of Grief."

relief—that I no longer had to worry about his wellbeing as he had now rested. It was a confusing feeling. I was however sure of the fact that I missed him. The fact remained, that my father, who had been my friend, was no more. He had suddenly been taken away from me. It is the thought of his sudden passing that caused much pain. I now know that the perception of death as sudden, potentially increases the risk of abnormal grief [11] (extreme and disabling grief).[12]

Nevertheless, one thing I had understood was that my father was ever ready to go and be with the Lord. He had expressed this many times over the years. In fact, like Apostle Paul in Philippians 1:23, dad openly shared that he preferred to go and be with the Lord in heaven, than to live very long. He had great anticipation for being with the Lord—after walking with and serving the Lord for many years. One thing that is striking around the circumstances of his death is that, weeks before his death, dad acted as though he somehow knew or sensed that he was about to go. He had hinted this to me and others in many ways, and on several occasions. He had given some final words to various people. He had notably travelled out of town to visit my brother, Heath. In the few days he was with Heath, dad hinted to him that his (dad) time to go and be with Lord had come. Heath did not comprehend the purpose of the visit until about a week later, soon after dad passed away. He was to later understand that dad had actually visited him to indirectly inform him and prepare him for his (dad) departure. Furthermore, some of my dad's prayer companions from his Thursday night prayer group were later to recount similar experiences. They particularly reported that three days before his passing on, though not very well in his

---

[11] Stroebe M. Schut H, and W, Stroebe W. "Health Outcomes of Bereavement." *Lancet*, (2007): 1960-73.

[12] Prigerson HG, Jacobs SC. "Traumatic Grief as a Distinct Disorder: A Rationale, Consensus Criteria, and a Preliminary Empirical Test. In: Stroebe MS, Hansson RO, Stroebe W, Schut H, Editors. Handbook of bereavement research: consequences, coping, and care. Washington (DC): American Psychological Association; 2001.

health—dad stood up in the prayer group. With a noticeable unique smile of joy, he joined in the worship of a particular hymn—that is themed around longing to go and be with the Lord in heaven.

Reflecting on such accounts helped me to move on. After I started to accept that he had gone, I begun to replay key life events and to think deeply about the whole situation. I started to evaluate, or more correctly, reflect on the whole situation more objectively— taking into account all that had happened, and how I was feeling. In all this, as a young maturing Christian, I was determined to allow God to be the source of strength and support. I took time to understand what the Word of God (Bible) said about my difficult situation. I particularly wanted to understand how the Word of God could influence my experience of loss. I was focused on the fact that God was the only one who could deal with my inner feelings. I had started to accept and come to terms with what had happened. I knew I could not reverse it. This led me to asking myself what I now consider a key question. It was not a **why** question—of why it had happened. It was rather the question, "what do I need to do, to make this situation more bearable?" The more I actively sought to understand the answer to this question, in line with the Word of God, the more I slowly altered my understanding of the situation.

I accepted the harsh reality that I my father was gone. I however wondered why the burden of grief was still there somewhere. I began to ponder on the thought that my father's passing on was not the problem I needed to address. I started thinking along the lines that the problem was more of how I was going to handle the loss, rather than the loss itself—which I could not reverse. This prompted me to read the Bible more—mostly around bereavement. I read some scriptures that I had read and also heard being preached before. However, this time my studying of these scriptures applied to my situation, so I paid more attention. This led me to new and deeper perspectives of what it means when a believer dies. I started meditating on these perspectives more strongly i.e. that: (1) those that die in the Lord are blessed, (2) they will rest from their hard work and (3) their good deeds will follow them (their good deeds will be accounted, for in future life—according to Revelation 14:13). This opened for a new understanding that dad was actually blessed, he had rested and that all he had done for the Lord would be rewarded in the life after death—at the Second Coming of Christ. This was a totally new way of looking at my loss—inspired by scripture.

I as well took time to understand the biblical thinking that for believers, to be absent from the body means to be present with the Lord (2 Corinthians 5:8). In fact, that is what dad had longed for, and for many years. I reflected, recognized and appreciated the fact that our father had worked very hard in his life. He had raised and cared for his family well. Most importantly, dad had faithfully served God for many years. He had moreover helped many people come to faith, discipled many others and offered life-changing pastoral support to many individuals and families. All these considerations helped me to come to a totally new approach and understanding of what the situation really was. It wasn't that of death, but that of a man who had completed his course of life, kept the faith (2 Timothy 4:7) and went home to rest. While the loss of my dad was painful, I knew that I needed to accept the loss and be strong. The Bible clearly teaches that we should mourn with hope (1 Thessalonians 4:13), understanding that those who "die" in the Lord will one day be resurrected in Christ. This became my focus and prayer, that the Lord would strengthen me in my Christian walk—so that I too would remain faithful to the end. From then, my prayers were directed at asking the Holy Spirit to help me to move on. The Lord helped me. I amazingly managed to move on. Of course I still have memories of both my parents. Nevertheless, they are all happy memories. Even as I write, I feel no pain revisiting these cherished memories. The more I reminisce on the good times I shared with my parents, the more I realize that I have to thank God for their lives. Particularly because they left me a legacy: a legacy of knowing & serving Christ. This is the greatest legacy any parent can ever give to their child, at least as far as I am concerned.

When I look back to the time that I was grieving, I was clouded by my loss. This is often the case when people are bereaved. We however should not dwell in that state for a very long time, as this may affect our healing and ability to move on. In my case, I overlooked some of the amazing things that God had done in and through dad's life. For instance, about a month before dad passed away (1998), he shared with me an amazing encounter he had with an angel, which I still find inspiring to this day.

Dad told me how around 1964 he had been hospitalized with Pulmonary Tuberculosis (TB) for about 12 months, in what I understood to be an infectious disease hospital ward, in Africa. During this time, he saw many people from the same ward die from TB—one after another. Other new patients would be admitted on the ward, but again, many of them would not survive the illness. Dad told me that while at the hospital, he started to wake-up around 4am daily, to go to a nearby bush to pray. This he did for a while. One day as he was praying, an angel appeared next to him. The angel then showed him a vision of an open grave, being closed. The angel then said to him that the illness should have taken his life, but God had heard his prayers—and had sent the angel to tell dad that his grave has now been closed, for "many years". Dad added that this encounter occurred before my brother Heath was born (that is before–1965), and that he had since not only had Heath, but 4 other children after that (including me). He explained that he had even seen Heath's two children, Winnie and Michael. After dad told me about this encounter, he went on to ask me, "don't you think that those *many years* have now passed?" He further asked me to count how many years he had lived since the encounter. I calculated and recognized that it was 34 years after the encounter (when we were having this conversation). Although my response to him was that I didn't think it was time for him to die yet, dad died the following month. This mirrors the famous and inspiring story of King Hezekiah in the Bible found in 2 Kings 20:1–60. Dad however got a better deal. While Hezekiah's life was extended by 15 years, dad's life was extended by 34 years. This is more than double the extension Hezekiah received! This brought a positive feeling to me, recognizing the great favor shown to dad.

I have shared this experience to show that my grief was clouding me so as to overlook the phenomenal life experiences dad had. I was for some time consumed with my loss. Of course I do understand that not everyone who is bereaved would have had exact experiences as mine. Here is a key lesson from my situation: losing a beloved one can cause us to forget some positive cherished memories about them. These are the memories that should actually cause us to smile, and give us motivation in life—even in our grief.

As I conclude this chapter, I would like to acknowledge that every situation of bereavement is unique—and will not present in the same way as with my father's death. It is also the case that sometime we lose a loved one who is not a Christian, where there is not the hope, comfort, or certainty that they have gone to a better place. Firstly, I would like to highlight that we do not always know what happens in someone's last moments. It is very possible that someone who has lived their life as a non-believer will turn to God at the last moment—unbeknown to others. A good example is the Bible story of a man who was dying on the cross alongside Jesus. This man acknowledged God and accepted Jesus as King in his last moment of life. Jesus responded to this by assuring the dying man a place in paradise (Luke 23:32–43). This shows that someone may take the opportunity to commit their life to Jesus at the moment of death—and be accepted into God's Kingdom. This can happen to any of our loved ones, and we may not be aware of it. We can therefore not be entirely sure that someone has not gone to paradise.

Secondly, even if our loved ones chose not to accept Christ to the point of death—the fact remains, that just having them in our lives was in itself a gift from God. Every life is a gift from God. God loves all people of the World (John 3:16)—that includes believers and non-believers. As a result, our memories of our loved ones should not only be about their faith, since not everyone in our lives is a believer. Our memories of our beloved should rather be all encompassing. This means that we should cherish the moments we shared with them, whether they believed or not. This gives us the opportunity to appreciate them, and consider having them in our lives a "blessing". This will help us to heal from the effects of bereavement.

Thirdly, I acknowledge that there are other more complex situations where someone may feel like they do not have good memories of their departed ones. This reminds me of a conversation I had with someone who was struggling to identify any positive memories of their mother who had passed away. This was because they hardly knew their mother. The mother had left her to be looked after by the grandmother, when she was a baby. The mother later reappeared in her life—only to pass away when the two were in the process of figuring out how to establish their relationship. She therefore felt a double impact of grief: (1) She struggled with the fact that her mum had left her when she was young—she was finding it hard to forgive her and (2) the hope of reconciliation was shattered by the mother's death. This meant that there was no hope of getting the answers as to why her mother had left her in the first place. In supporting her, I encouraged her to consider the possibility that her mum may have experienced some complex challenges at the time. Challenges that made her leave her as a child. I further asked her to take time and to consider that while she did not know her mother well, she could try and view her mother as an instrument that God used to bring her into the world—to fulfill the purpose that God has planned for her in life. This may help someone in a similar situation.

CHAPTER 6

Theological Reflection

In the previous chapter I highlighted how reflecting on the death of my father, theologically, enabled me to overcome grief. While I could not prevent my father's death, I reflected on the situation through the eyes of the Bible, coupled with prayer. This helped me to move on. We get more from reflecting on situations if we understand the underpinnings of reflection. This chapter is set to explore how *theological reflection* can be consciously applied in a variety of life-challenging situations. Christians can effectively use *theological reflection* to reflect on their everyday life situations, in order to have better experiences of bad situations. To help understand this—in order to put it into practice, I will discuss the principle of *theological reflection* in a more simplified way.

I will start by explaining the general principle of reflecting on actions—as it is the basis of *theological reflection*. The approach of looking at (reflecting on) actions and experiences, in order to improve future practice and experiences is a key aspect of contemporary professional practice. Within professional practice, reflective practice has been defined as "the ability to reflect on an action so as to engage in a process of continuous learning".[13] Likewise, the

---

[13] Schon, Donald, *The Reflective Practitioner: How Professionals Think in Action*. New York: Basic Books, 1983.

Christian journey is a process of continuous learning. The approach of continuous learning through reflecting on situations and practice that is common in the professional world, should be emulated. Believers can and should use the principles of reflective practice with great benefit, when encountering life-challenges. As Christians, we should consider life-challenges as opportunities to reflect on scripture—in order to improve how we respond to life situations (i.e. in ways that are more consistent with biblical truth). *Theological reflection* can therefore be applied in an individual's Christian life as a means of seeking solutions or Divine comfort, in times of difficulties.

Theological reflection describes the process of learning directly from our experiences (Trokan, 2013:145).[14] This is achieved through the use various sources—of which scripture and the situation itself are integral.[15] Reflecting on life situations through the eyes of scripture (the Word) will make room for Godly solutions. It will further enable believers to seek and yield to Godly support and comfort in the face of enduring challenging situations. *Theological reflection* is a reflective search, and a way of doing theology, which starts from experiences of life, and leads to searching into our faith for deeper meaning.[16] Scripture (the Word of God) plays the role of strengthening Christian faith—and it is through the prayerful interpretation of scripture that this deeper meaning (seeing the situation from God's perspective) is found.

It is important that we understand the depth of the meaning of the term, *Word*, as used in the New Testament. The original Greek (LOGOS), translated to, *Word*, in sections of the English Bible, has

[14] Trokan, John "Models of Theological Reflection: Theory and Praxis, Catholic Education": *A Journal of Inquiry and Practice*, Volume 1, Issue 2, (July 2013):144-58.

[15] Mowat, John and Harriet Swinton. "*Practical Theology and Qualitative Research.*"

[16] McAlpine, Kathleen, *Ministry That Transforms: A Contemplative Process of Theological Reflection*. Minnesota: Liturgic Press, 2009.

a deep meaning. In the religious philosophical understanding of the time when the gospel of John was written, "LOGOS was one of the purest and most general concepts of that ultimate Intelligence, Reason, or Will that is called God" (Tenney, 1977:62).[17] This understanding mirrors the presentation of the Word, as God, in John's Gospel (1:1–18). The Word is equated with God—the essence of God. The *Word* is an instrument that God uses to reveal Himself, and His principles to mankind. As a result, reflecting on scripture—is drawing from God Himself. Drawing from scripture is effectively drawing from God's *Intelligence, Reason and Will* in the life-situations we face. Difficult situations therefore present believers with the opportunity to search into the wisdom of scripture, in order to: (1) understand the situation theologically (from God's perspective)—beyond the view of what it looks like in the natural and (2) seek guidance on how to respond to the situation.

I acknowledge that reflecting on situations is not an instantaneous magical formula that will take away all of life's problems. Depending on the situation, it will likely be a process. The process of reflecting through the loss of my father was not instantaneous. It took me some months to arrive at the new perspective (biblical) —being at peace with the loss. It required a process of considering and accepting that while dad was no longer present with me, he had gone to a better place, and had rested. It sometimes takes time before one feels ready or able to start reflecting on a difficult situation. It is a matter of finding an appropriate moment. The results of reflecting on my situation, through the eyes of scripture, have however been long lasting. 19 years on, I am more reassured through the Word of God that life on earth is not eternal. Secondly, I am encouraged that while we should mourn the death of our beloved who die in the

---

[17] Tenney, Merril C, *John the Gospel of Belief: An Analytic Study of the Text*, Grand Rapids: Eerdmans, 1977.

Lord (believers), we should do so with the hope that they will be resurrected at the second coming of Jesus (1 Thessalonians 4:13 –18). Thirdly, I am reassured that blessed are the dead who die in the Lord, for they will rest from their hard work, and that their good deeds will follow them (Revelations 14:13).

CHAPTER 7

Asking the Right Questions

This chapter continues where we left in chapter 6. Now that we have explained the essence of reflecting on situations theologically, I move on to explain how this can be put in practice. Asking questions is an important aspect of gaining more understanding of life situations. Harvard Business School Professor Robert Simons coined that business leaders can't develop and execute effective strategy without first gathering the right information— through asking the right questions.[18] This makes sense. Asking questions is common in all areas of life. People often ask questions when faced with difficult situations. This usually occurs in the mind. When a situation is unbearable—where there is no hope of coming out of the situation soon or when a situation is longer than we comfortably can bear. One may ask, *"why is this happening to me"?* This is an important question.

Why is (or did) this Happen?

One day my wife and I visited someone who had lost their spouse to pray and support them. They appreciated our visit, which helped them in two ways. First, this gave them the opportunity to have a

---

[18] Simons, Robert, "Seven Strategy Questions: A Simple Approach for Better Execution". Boston: *Harvard Business Review Press*, 2010.

general social conversation with and laughter. Second, they were able to share and open up about some challenges they were experiencing. I was able to support and advise on some of the issues. It is common for people who are bereaved to be lonely. Their friends and those close to them may avoid them or avoid discussing issues that pertain to their experience. This is because they may not know what to say to them. It is true that it can be daunting, particularly for lay people (family and friends), to initiate deep discussions that counsellors and trained ministers may be more equipped to ask. Nevertheless, during our visit I asked them how they were was coping with the situation, a few months on. They openly shared that it was difficult to adjust to the situation, but that they were coping better than before. I further sensitively inquired about their spiritual wellbeing. It was reassuring that they continued to trust the Lord for comfort, and they had not stopped trusting or worshipping God. It is encouraging to know that many of God's children will continue to love and trust Him in the midst of difficult situations. They however went on to reveal how they had grappled with an unanswered question; a question that I have been asked a number of times by those who lose a loved one. I actually remember my dad asking the same question when mum passed away: "*Why did she have to go now?*"

This is one question I could never answer. They were of course not expecting me to have an answer. This was just a way of venting thoughts and emotions, which manifested as a result of deep distress. I did not offer an answer to this question. I was in fact honest, and said that it was difficult to understand why this had happened (from a human perceptive). It always is. While we were all unable to specifically answer that question, their asking the question offered us the opportunity to explore it together. It presented me the opportunity to find a more effective way to support them. This included the reading of scriptures, which highlighted that; (1) those who die in the Lord are in a better place and (2) they will come back to life and (3) the Lord is a source of comfort to those that mourn (Matthew 5:4). While this does not explain the why question, these assurances provided a source of comfort, in this case, as in many others. While it is very hard to cope after the death of someone close, who is a Christian, there is a positive perspective to their departure—that there is the hope of seeing them again in glory (heaven)—where there is no hunger, thirst or crying (Revelations 7:16 –17). The Lord's comfort is not only limited to when our Christian loved ones die. He is equally a source of comfort when we lose those we love—who are not believers, as already explained.

CHAPTER 8

Do I Have Control Over What Happens in My Life?

The question of how much control an individual has over what happens in their life is an important theological question—one that has no simple answer to it. I have already discussed the complexity of human life in preceding chapters. I, however, want to highlight one important factor that makes life more complex, which I have reserved to discuss in this chapter in greater depth. Three entities influence our experiences of life that we need to be consciously aware of. These broadly manifest at three levels: (1) Divine influences, (2) human influences and (3) influences from evil forces. This leads us to the understanding that some difficult situations we encounter in life, are respectively; designed or allowed by God, some are as a result of human choices and actions (self or others), and still others are caused by Satan. This notion is well supported in scripture as will emerge in this chapter. It is therefore very important for believers to grasp this fact. This will empower them to explore life's disconcerting situations with more insight, and furthermore equip them to respond to the situations more effectively. We will look at each of these three influences in turn.

Human Influences – *The power of our choices, decisions and actions*

It is fact that life is about constantly making choices and decisions. Our actions are largely a result of the things we chose and decide to do. To fully comprehend this, just consider how many choices and decisions you make each day. I attempted to evaluate myself on this. I started from the moment I woke up in the morning, and realized that I immediately made the decision of when to actually get out of bed. Following that, I decided on whether or not to do my daily push ups that morning before bathing, or later, after work. I further had to decide whether to have breakfast at home or at work, what to have for breakfast, what I was going wear to work and what time to leave home. These are just some of the decisions I made just in the first hour into the day. As the day progressed, I made other numerous decisions, pertaining to my work, my family life, the ministry etc. The truth of the matter is that, I actually lost count of the number of choices and decisions I had made in the first 3 hours of the day. I gave up counting. From this reflection of my life, which I think reflects that of many others in the world—it is clear that making choices and decisions is a large part of our lives. Human beings are thus decision-making beings. Making decisions and choices on the other hand produces actions—and actions produce results. So my choice to eat Weetabix breakfast cereal (which is by the way one of my favorite breakfast cereals), meant I had to prepare it and subsequently eat it. Because I had eaten a filling breakfast, this influenced how long I had to wait before eating the next meal.

While we are able to make many effective judgements and decisions, science has helped us understand that there are many factors, which affect our decision-making. This became clearer to me when I took up the Leadership Decision Making Executive course at Harvard Kennedy School in Boston, MA. I was to explore a whole new world of decision science. I was exposed to research and experiments (some of which I participated in) that effectively demonstrate how our judgement and decision-making is inherently imperfect. Of course we are humans, and we are not perfect. The aim of the program was to impart a framework that enables participants to identify some factors that affect human judgement, and how best to mitigate them—in order to make decisions better.

Nevertheless, the decisions and choices we ourselves and others make, impact on our lives. Some decisions and choices have greater impact in our lives than others. For example, my decision to read for a Master's Degree while working full time and leading a church, impacted on a number of aspects for my life. This included a significant impact on my finances, a strain in balancing my time in the three most important domains of my life: family, ministry and work. So while this decision affected me, it also affected those around me. I am always reminded of when I was working on the dissertation for the master's degree, which was by the way, my decision. My then two-year-old daughter Alicia had come to know that my being on the computer meant that I was busy. Unfortunately (for her), this happened a lot. She would occasionally come into the study room to check if daddy was busy or free to play. Upon seeing me on the computer, she would say "Oh daddy is still busy.", and leave the room. So my decision to pursue post graduate studies impacted on play time with my daughter. However, after this happened a few times, I realized how it was affecting my little angel. From then on, I made sure (*made a decision*) to play with her till she was tired, before working on my academic work. The point I make here is that, the decisions and choices that we and others make are powerful forces. They have the potential to significantly affect our lives and that of others.

Our life choices and decisions will have the potential to enormously influence and affect all areas of our lives, including but not limited to health and wellbeing, relationships, finances, education, spirituality etc. You, as a matter of fact, have a significant amount of control over your life and destiny. It is therefore important to understand that sometimes *things go wrong in your life because of you*! Being human, we are liable to make wrong and sometimes foolish choices and decisions, which negatively affect us. There however is the temptation for believers to attribute every bad experience in life to Satan. There's no doubt that Satan is really a 'bad guy'. The Bible is clear on the evil nature and intentions of Satan. However, although it may feel good to blame Satan for everything that goes wrong, this does not resolve our situations. While the Bible is clear about the influences of Divine (Godly) and evil (satanic) forces, it also highlights and demonstrates the power of the human factor, called *freewill* (see Genesis 2:16 –17, Deuteronomy 30:19 –20, James 1:13 –15). Freewill "voluntary choice or decision"[19] is also described as, "The power of making free choices unconstrained by external agencies."[20] It refers to the God given autonomy by which humans exercise the expression of choice. It is demonstrated by "the ability to decide what to do independently of any outside influence".[21] Having free will is obviously a great gift given to us by God. Having freewill, however, means that there will be instances where we make choices and decisions that will affect our lives either positively or negatively. God's system of accountability, reward and judgement would be meaningless if everything we do was controlled by God or Satan. It would be absurd for God to judge or reward people, if they were not responsible for their choices, decisions and actions. In reality, however, the greater part of our lives is influenced by the human factor. The human factor also impacts on our experience of, and relationship with the Divine (God). As an example, salvation is a result of a choice and decision. "Because, if you confess with your mouth that Jesus is Lord and believe in your heart that God

---

[19] "Merriam Webster Dictionary." Accessed September 15, 2017. https://www.merriam-webster.com/dictionary/free%20will.

[20] "Cambridge Advanced Learners Dictionary", Third Edition. Cambridge: Cambridge University Press, 2008.571.

[21] "Cambridge Dictionary." Accessed September 15, 2017. https://www.dictionary.cambridgeorg/dictionary/english/free-will.

raised him from the dead, you will be saved. For with the heart one believes and is justified, and with the mouth one confesses and is saved" (Romans 10:9-10 ESV). In essence, our God given freedom (*freewill*) paradoxically works out for the benefit or detriment of our experiences—depending on the choices we make.

Here is a scenario, to help demonstrate this point. Let's consider someone who has a driving job, who decides to drink excess alcohol, drives a car under the influence of alcohol and eventually causes a road traffic accident. A variety of negative consequences can arise from this scenario. These will include causing injury/death to self or others, and being convicted under the law, which may result in imprisonment and or driving ban. Each of these consequence may trigger yet another chain of consequences e.g. health issues such as Post-traumatic Stress Disorder (PTSD) and losing their job and associated loss of income. These consequences may affect the lives and livelihood of the individual and their family. The question is therefore, who is to blame— is it Satan or the individual who carried out the legally, morally and biblically wrong decision? We should not always blame Satan for every negative experience. Of course it is true that Satan takes opportunities to worsen a situation like this. The point I highlight here is that human choices, decisions and actions can lead to life difficulties. It is therefore helpful that if and when going through a challenging situation, one should take care to deeply reflect on the situation—to try and identify the human contribution to the situation. That will be a significant step in rectifying problems. Evaluation of situations will also help avoid or minimize the chances of us repeating the same mistakes. But this starts with the individual taking responsibility for their actions—followed by true repentance (where sin is involved) to allow the effective working of the Holy Spirit. This principle is applicable in a variety of situations, and is not limited to the hypothetical scenario presented. This reflection should be reinforced by prayer. In fact, one should pray and ask God to give them the power and wisdom to correct their mistakes, and then take the necessary actions to rectify the mistakes.

Taking Responsibility of Decisions Without Self-Condemning

To balance this view, it is important to highlight that taking responsibility of one's actions should not be seen in the light of self-condemnation. Some individuals struggle with self-blame more than others. When things go wrong, they will be more disposed to blame one person, and one person only—themselves. This will however cause them to see no hope for the future. It also robs them of the opportunity to discern the situation more deeply, and explore what other factors could have contributed to the situation. While it is true that we can make some errors in judgement, we should be careful not to censure ourselves for situations and outcomes we are not responsible for—or for other people's decisions and actions. Self-blaming and blaming others for our actions, are two extreme reactions to situations.

Self-blaming and self-condemning tendencies are as negative as wrongfully blaming others for our actions. If not managed well, this may lead to more serious psychological disorders. I have encountered individuals who struggle with self-blame in a variety of circumstances, in my pastoral role. I will however give one of the many examples. This involved supporting an individual going through a marriage breakdown—after being deserted by their spouse. I should highlight here that I am not saying that the spouse that leaves is necessarily responsible for the marriage breakdown. No. I have in fact known spouses leave their homes for safety reasons—where leaving the home was the only safe option they had i.e. where extreme violence was involved. The point I am making is nonetheless that some faithful individuals have lived with severe depression, which is exacerbated by persistently blaming themselves for the wrong or selfish decisions of others.

Self-blaming for a Marriage Breakdown: (A real life situation)

The scenario involves a woman who had admittedly said, "Pastor, my husband is a wonderful person—and I'm leaving him not because of what he has or not done—but because of my selfish desires to try out life as a single woman". She had opened up to her husband about this—long before they approached me for support. The marriage eventually broke down, and she consequently moved away to start a new life in another country. She however left the children with the man. After she left, the man became so depressed—which was not surprising, given the situation. Because he could not cope, he and the children went to live with his parents for some time. Luckily, his parents lived in the same city. For a very long time, he blamed himself for his wife's actions (leaving). Although he could not find what he had done to drive her away, he became consumed by searching for what he could have done wrong. This went on for years. This progressed into blaming himself for the marriage breakdown. He exhibited traits of *behavioral self-blame*—where he felt he should have done something differently, and therefore felt at fault. At other times, he disclosed having what I was later to understand as *characterological self-blame*—believing that something was inherently wrong with him, which caused him to deserve to be deserted.[22] He however found some great relief from antidepressants for many years. Nevertheless, in moments where he went into a state of self-blaming mode, he would relapse into depression, and this became a cycle. He nonetheless was receiving medical and psychological support. As I ministered to him from a spiritual (Christian faith) perspective, I was also determined to help him to explore his own situation, in relation to his faith

---

[22] Janoff-Bulman R. "Characterological Versus Behavioral Self-blame: Inquiries into Depression and Rape." *J Pers Soc Psychol* 37, no.10. (October 1979):1798-809.

(Christian). I firmly believe that God can heal and restore people's situations instantly. I have in fact experienced God perform instant healings, breakthroughs, and divine interventions of various sorts in my personal and ministry life (numerous times). However, in some situations God allows for us to minister to the thoughts and emotions of others, as a process. As a result, through prayer and a lot of counselling, the man in the scenario eventually realised that self-blaming for something he had no control over was his biggest challenge.

This was a breakthrough. It made my ministry "strategy" (direction) for this situation clearer. My objective was to support the individual to break this cycle of self-blame. This included a lot of reference to scriptures that show that Christ has paid for our freedom. I continued supporting him through making prayers specifically directed at asking the Lord to relieve him from the struggle of self-blame. In our prayers (that included fasting), we also included focus on firmly denouncing satanic influence in the situation. As I have highlighted above, Satan can take opportunity of situations that are already bad, in an effort to destroy our lives. In summary, through much prayer and application of the Word of God, he overcame the situation. It is with the help of the Holy Spirit that he was able to overcome self-blame. For a long time since; he has been free from needing antidepressants. This is an example of how we can and should be praying for anything and everything that challenges us as believers. If we believe God can heal physical ailments, we should also believe that He has the power to heal all our inflictions (Psalm 103:3). That includes emotional & psychological 'ailments'.

Avoid Blaming Others for Your Misfortune

It is often easy or natural to blame our parents, spouse, friends, relatives, the devil or even God, when things go wrong. It is true that the choices and decisions of others, particularly those close to us, can affect us. We must, however, be conscious to avoid wrongly blaming others for our situations. By way of example, let's consider an employer who lawfully and 'fairly' terminates an employee's employment—for clear gross misconduct. Is it not natural to overlook the actions of the employee that led to the consequence, and blame the employer or manager for terminating the job? It is often the case that when we are in distress, our ability to be objective is clouded by our emotions. It, however, occurs that when a lot of time is taken blaming others, little or no time will be used to explore possible solutions to problems, or to ask the Lord for guidance and help in prayer. Reflecting on situations should always involve prayer. Effective prayer enables us to be more open to the influence of Holy Spirit. Prayer will also help us to deal with bitterness towards others that may arise from our experience and or perception of situations. We may become wrongly angry towards others because we have not taken time to prayerfully seek to understand the situation. The Bible is clear that bitterness and anger, if unaddressed, will lead to sin (Ephesians 4:26: 4:31). Sin hinders the relationship with God. Even when others wrong us, and their actions affect our situations, we should learn to forgive. The Bible guides us: "Bear with each other and forgive one another if any of you has a grievance against someone. Forgive as the Lord forgave you" (Colossians 3:13 NIV). The chapter on prayer will provide further guidance on praying for forgiveness. Admittedly, it is not always easy to forgive. With that in mind, I recommend anyone struggling with unforgiveness to seek support from a Christian minister and or to look for Christian literature and resources that specifically address the issue of unforgiveness. Unforgiveness is a burden in itself, and can compound situations that are already difficult. Moreover, the Lord expects us to forgive.

The Adam Syndrome

There are also situations where people make joint decisions that will result in problems. Even in such situations, it is easy to blame the other person, and forget your own contribution to the problem. One classic biblical example is found in the narrative of Adam and Eve, in the book of Genesis. When Adam disobeyed the commandment not to eat the fruit from the tree of knowledge of good and evil, God asked him a direct question, "......Have you eaten from the tree that I commanded you not to eat from?" (Genesis 3:11 NIV). In his response, Adam apparently blames Eve (for giving him the fruit) and God (for giving him Eve); "The woman you put here with me—she gave me some fruit from the tree, and I ate it" (Genesis 3:12 NIV). Adam overlooks his error and blames his accomplice. Thankfully, God was the ultimate judge—and not Adam. There is no doubt that Adam was the main actor in this drama of disobedience. That is the reason why God asked Adam about the eating of the forbidden fruit. The instruction not to eat the fruit was given to him directly, before Eve came into the picture (Genesis 2:15 –17). After addressing the snake and the woman for their contribution in the disobedience, God turned to Adam and said, "Because you listened to your wife and ate fruit from the tree about which I commanded you, 'You must not eat from it...'" (3:1 NIV). Romans 5:12 –14 highlights that death came to all humans through the sin of Adam.

Evil Influences—Satanic forces

I have explained at length the fact that some of the situations we face in life are direct consequences of our life-choices, decisions and actions. It is also important to understand that some situations will arise as a result of factors beyond our choices, decisions and actions—but as result of satanic influences. There are different views on this subject. I will highlight two 'extreme' perspectives on this subject. On one hand, there is the view that believers are 'fully' immune to Satanic powers and influences—and that Satan and his power and influence should not to be a concern for the believers—and should not deserve any mention or attention in our lives and prayers. On the other hand, there is the direct opposite view that considers the believer's life is in danger of Satanic powers and influences—to the point of almost advocating that a larger proportion of Christian attention and prayers should be directed at combating Satan's forces and adversity—causing some believers to live in a state anxiety and fear. Every negative experience of life such as sin, conflict and each and every problem or undesired situation is consequently considered an outcome of Satan's direct attack.

If we examine these two premises, we can see that they both have some, and only some, elements of biblical truth. I can therefore see how some Christians have come to embrace these views. The fact of the matter is, however, that both views are largely distant from the teaching of the Bible. What we have in these two extreme views is that one view (the former) will under-emphasise the influence and impact of evil forces as presented in the Bible; and other (the latter) will magnify satanic power—beyond how it is presented in the Bible. Both these views will impede on how we are to understand and respond to life challenging situations as I will elaborate below.

Can Satan Affect the Life of a Believer?

The Bible warns believers on this question: "Stay alert! Watch out for your great enemy, the devil. He prowls around like a roaring lion, looking for someone to devour" (1Pe 5:8 NLT). We are also enlightened that "…….we are not fighting against flesh-and-blood enemies, but against evil rulers and authorities of the unseen world, against mighty powers in this dark world, and against evil spirits in the heavenly places" (Ephesians 6:12 NLT). These passages (representative of many other Bible passages) highlight the existence of satanic conflict. These texts, particularly Ephesians, present satanic forces as manifesting in a form which the human eye cannot see, and the human mind cannot fathom. Here the Bible explains that Satan's forces and influence converges with and impacts our lives. It also, importantly, elaborates that the real conflict occurs at a non-physical (unseen) level. This is important to understand.

Going back to the two extreme views of satanic influence we discussed above, it is important we underline that the warnings in 1Peter 5:8 and Ephesians 6:12 are directed to the church (believers). This is contrary to the view that believers are 'fully' immune to satanic powers and influences—and that the manifestation of Satan, his power and influence should not be a concern for the believer. Through these (and other) scriptures, God enlightens believers on: (1) the existence of the devil, (2) the devil's ill-intentions for mankind (Revelations 12:7 –12), (3) the fact that the devil operates supernaturally and (4) the fact that believers are not immune to his influences and attacks. Most importantly, God's Word calls on believers to resist Satan's adversity. The less conscious of Satan's influence we are, the more we become open to the influences of evil, even without knowing. That places us in a position of weakness to act against the operations of evil—even though God has already equipped us to overcome them..

The spiritual forces of evil have the potential to affect us at different levels—i.e. physically, mentally, psychologically and socially. Mark 5:1–20 gives us a good example of this. In this passage, Jesus encounters a man who is under the attack and influence of an evil spirit. This resulted in the man: (1) being mentally challenged—that he lived at a grave site, which consequently isolated him from society (vs 3), (2) becoming emotionally distressed—and always crying out (vs 5) and (3) harming himself—physically cutting himself with stones (vs 5).

Also, Mark 9 presents the story of a boy who could not hear or speak—who also presented with seizures. When asked to heal the boy, Jesus responded by confronting an evil spirit that was the source of the situation saying: "Listen, you spirit that makes this boy unable to hear and speak," I command you to come out of this child and never enter him again!" (vs. 25 NLT). Again here we see that evil (satanic) forces are real, and have the potential to affect our lives, naturally. It is reassuring to know through this passage that although Satan's power has the potential to harm humans, our Lord Jesus conquers Satan.

Let's take one more example—this time of how Satan can afflict someone who has a good relationship with God with suffering. A lot can be learnt from this. After Satan set to tempt Job to denounce God, God allowed him (Satan). God said, "Very well, then, everything he has is in your power, but on the man himself do not lay a finger" (Job 1:12 NIV). God therefore gave Satan access into all of Jobs' life— but denied him the power to kill Job (1:12). This resulted in Satan having access to Job's life and possessions. Satan consequently caused Job to lose his assets (cattle & donkeys), his servants to be killed and for all his children to die at once (1:13 –20). From this, we learn that Satan's influence on human life may present as natural situations that can be seen and explained in the natural. While it is clear here that Satan was the force behind Job's misfortunes, the death of his children can be explained as natural accidental occurrence—that occurred from an accidental collapse of a building, due to strong winds. This raises the question: how many things happen to us that are caused by the devil, which we have not taken time to pray over—to combat Satan?

Exposing Satan Empowers the Believer

In highlighting this fundamental biblical insight, my aim is not to glorify the powers of Satan. I am rather exposing him—so that believers are more informed of his ways, and thereby become more empowered to overcome him. There should therefore be no confusion about the fact that God has the ultimate Power—Power far greater than the powers of Satan! Believers should also be aware that God our Father has equipped believers through His son Jesus (who overcame Satan) to overcome satanic forces and influences. Jesus delegated His power to believers—so that we too can exercise the same privilege of God's power to combat and inhibit the influences of evil powers—that can affect humans in a number of ways. In Luke 10:19 Jesus explains how He gave his followers the authority to overcome all the enemy's powers. In Mark 16:7 Jesus explicitly empowers believers to miraculously expel demonic (satanic) oppressions and influences from people who are oppressed by them, and to heal the sick through His name. Through our faith in Jesus, the Holy Spirit enables us to employ spiritual methods and principles outlined in the Bible to overcome Satan (1 Corinthians 10:3 – 4). As Christians, we should be aware of the fact that Satan exists, and that he can potentially inflict harm on our lives, in different ways. More than this, we should know we can (and should) defeat Satan by employing Godly ways that are outlined in the Bible. This will include making specific prayers to combat Satan's forces that may be set against us—when we sense or suspect his attacks on us. This is contrary to the view that Christians should live in fear and anxiety of what Satan could do to us. We should instead actively exercise our God-given privilege and authority over Satan's powers and evil intentions. It is comforting to know that this phenomenal privilege is not restricted to Jesus and His early followers. It is available to believers even today. I am glad that I also experience and exercise this privilege. This leads me to share two of many real-life examples of this experience in order to put this insight into perspective.

Satan's Defeat in a Situation of Illness (*real life situation*)

One evening I received a call from an individual requesting for prayer support. They had been to the hospital suffering a sudden serious headache, back pain and acute pain in one of their eyes. They said that they had been discharged following some tests that did not reveal any abnormalities except for "a blood clot and a swollen vessel at the back of the eye". They had been sent home with a medical eye patch (cover) and some eye drops. They, however, reported experiencing a severe headache, shivering and feeling cold, in spite of it being mid-summer— and that they were wearing a sweater and a jacket. I took time to pray with them over the phone, asking the Lord to heal them. As I prayed, I also included and exercised my God given authority—denouncing any evil spirit that may have been influencing ill health. At this point I was not certain of any such influence. The prayer went on for about a quarter of an hour. At the end of the prayer, the individual reported that that they felt much better. The headache in particular had instantly resolved. I could tell from their voice that they felt better during the prayer—as they joined me in the prayer, midway. After the prayer, I asked them to continue trusting God for total healing and to continue praying on their own in their own time. We agreed to meet up for prayer in the next few days if the problem had not resolved.

When we next met, the symptoms were still present. They were struggling to walk or stand. They were wearing a heavy jacket and shivering although it was mid-summer. One of their eyes was patched. I prayed for her as she sat on the floor. As I gently placed my hand on their head in prayer, they gently laid on the floor. This is a common experience of the manifest presence of the power of God that sometimes overwhelms the body and consciousness. However, it was at that point that I sensed through the Holy Spirit that their situation was as a result of satanic influence—and that with prayer, they would be healed of all their symptoms that very moment. At this point, they were still laid on the floor, semi-conscious. I openly shared with other believers present, the spiritual revelations that our friend's situation was something that God would heal instantly—if we prayed, asking Lord to get rid of the evil influence that was influencing the illness (as we saw in Mark 16:17). To summarize this story, we prayed collectively as I placed my hands on them, as in Mark 16:18 and Luke 4:40. After about 5 minutes of prayer, I again received insight from the Holy Spirit that the evil spirit causing the illness had left, and that their health had been restored. Suddenly, the individual sat up with no assistance. I asked them how they were feeling. Before responding to me, they started to remove the heavy jacket they were wearing. They were now evidently profusely sweating. The big smile on their face was visible to everyone looking at them. They carried on smiling with tears of joy running down their cheeks. We all could not help but collectively praise and appreciate Jesus who had yet again performed a miracle of healing amongst us. After that, the individual stood on their own, with no one supporting them to stand—unlike when they came for prayers. They willingly shared their experience with those who were present. I sometimes offer people the opportunity to share their experiences with others if they are willing. This is not to show that I or anyone in our ministry has powers, but is an opportunity for our Lord Jesus to be glorified publicly, and at the same time offering hope and encouragement to others. It demonstrates that Jesus still intervenes in our lives today, through the Holy Spirit. It is also the same reason that we pray collectively in such moments, so that no one individual gets credit for Jesus' work.

Nevertheless, they explained to everyone that the backache, headache, pain in the eye together and the feeling of cold and shivering had instantly vanished. They went on to say that they were only keeping their eye dressing on because they had earlier in the morning put some eye drops, and that it would not be a pleasant sight if they removed the dressing in public. I however advised that they go back to be reviewed by the doctors as planned. A few days later, they called to advise me they had been reviewed medically. The pain and discomfort had not re-emerged. They also said that it was reported that the clot and the swollen vessel in the eye had resolved.

Satan Defeated in the Healing of a Lump on the Throat (A real life situation)

One Sunday as I was concluding preaching in our church, I noticed a certain lady (visitor) walk into the meeting. After the meeting ended, she approached me, introduced herself and apologized for walking into the meeting late. She however explained that she had travelled by bus from another city. She knew someone in our church who had encouraged her to attend our meetings and take the opportunity to receive prayers concerning a long-term situation she was going through. As she was explaining her situation, the Lord gave me the insight that she was under oppression from an evil spirit. I obviously didn't mention this to her. I had only met her on this occasion. I therefore did not know how much she understood about the Bible and its teaching on the existence and activity of evil forces. We agreed and planned to meet at a later date for prayers.

The lady consequently attended one of our Friday evening prayer meetings. During prayer time, my wife and I prayed over her. Just as we laid our hands upon her, she manifested in a 'demon possessed state.' This is best understood as an activity of demonic powers that may temporarily take control of a person's mental and bodily capabilities from the inside.[23] This commonly manifests when God's Power becomes active in an individual's life, usually during prayer, affecting and displacing the evil forces that sometimes invade people's lives. The 'burning effect' of God's Power on demonic forces sometimes result in the demons in an individual's (host) life using their body and mind in an attempt to resist or react to God's Powerful presence. Some of the manifestations are violent. It is important to understand that this is a spiritual manifestation that is using someone's body and mind to react to God's presence, and not the individual themselves. While unpleasant to witness, such manifestations may help us to realise: (1) the presence of demonic forces in someone's life and (2) that God's Power is acting against those forces.

Nevertheless, the manifestation with this lady was quite violent. We supported her and continued praying for her to be set free from the evil spirit. After sometime of prayer, the spirit left her, and she became settled. Shortly after the meeting, she told us that she had not

---

[23] Catholic Spiritual Direction. *Differences in Demon possession, Mental Illness, Depression.* Accessed January 18, 2018. https://www.spiritualdirection. com/2017/11/1/6/differences-in-demon-possession-mental-ilness-or-depression

felt as free in her mind and body in a very long time. She explained that she felt as if something heavy had been removed from her. Early the next morning she rung me and said that she was amazed by the power of God that had touched her life during prayer. She said that she had for many years felt as though she had a lump on her throat that had never been medically identified or resolved—that irritated her. This caused her to cough in between sentences. She said that from the time after prayer the previous night, her throat had been unbelievably clear, and that her faith in God had been strengthened.

Unsure if Satan is Involved in Your Situation?

One of the questions I usually get asked when discussing this subject is: "How do I pray if I am not sure if evil forces are involved in my situation?" Wouldn't it be good if we always knew when satanic powers are involved in our situations? Unfortunately, we do not always know. We do not always get the spiritual insight (revelation) to know if our situation is as a result of an attack from Satan. That does not however mean that we should not do anything about it. Rather, we should pray for all the situations that we encounter, asking the Lord to help us. Since the Bible is clear that Satan can affect our lives in a number of ways, our prayers should include condemning and confronting any satanic influence or activity that may be involved in our difficult situations. This will be covered in greater detail in the chapter that discusses prayer. I will however conclude this section highlighting that satanic influences and inflictions will be overcome, when we actively confront them in prayer, in the name of Jesus.

Divine Influences – *the Godly influence*

It is very reassuring to know that God through the Holy Spirit intervenes in our lives for our good. God's influence and intervention in our lives is always for the best outcome. This does however not mean that God's will or plan is only manifest in our lives when things are good. There are times when things go wrong in our lives and God uses those circumstances to bring about something positive according to His purpose and plan. So, while nature or Satan may be the source of some negative experiences, God can sometimes allow or use those instances to bring about His plans and purposes. While such experiences are unpleasant, they bring about more positive outcomes—positive to the point that it overshadows the negative experiences of the situation. We will begin by examining one of Apostle Paul's situations to understand this more clearly

> Therefore, to keep me from being too elated, a thorn was given to me in the flesh, a messenger of Satan to torment me, to keep me from being too elated. Three times I appealed to the Lord about this, that it would leave me, but he said to me, 'My grace is sufficient for you, for power is made perfect in weakness.' So, I will boast all the more gladly of my weaknesses, so that the power of Christ may dwell in me. Therefore I am content with weaknesses, insults, hardships, persecutions, and calamities for the sake of Christ; for whenever I am weak, then I am strong. (2 Corinthians 12:7-10 NRSV).

This is not a simple passage to understand, particularly when seeking encouragement for a difficult situation. I will take time to explain the passage in order to show how inspiring this passage is, particularly when facing life-challenges—in the Lord. There is not much detail in the passage about the exact nature of the situation that Paul experienced, which is described in scripture as a 'thorn in the flesh'. It is however clear that this was an 'undesirable situation' that significantly affected him in some way. The situation must have caused worry and distress for Paul.

The first thing we learn here is that Paul did not endure distress in isolation; rather, he asked the Lord for help. He pleaded with the Lord (earnestly prayed)—asking Him "three times" to take the situation away. As discussed before, the Bible encourages us to pray to God for all our needs. The second thing we learn is that the Lord responded to Paul. God will respond to our prayers, one way or the other. It is important to understand that God's response is not always dramatic. Sometimes times it is through an inner sense of comfort and peace. This is when one feels and is overwhelmed by the sense that the Lord has heard our prayers—even when one does not see any physical manifestation or immediate change in the situation. This will be the working of the Holy Spirit. God is Spirit, and He operates spiritually. Nevertheless, the third lesson in the passage comes from the fact that while Satan was the instrument (causing agent) of Paul's affliction (12:7), and that Paul had prayed to God for help—God allowed the situation to continue, for a greater purpose. This is similar to Job's situation that has been highlighted in previous chapters. This is of course not easy to understand or accept.

God's Plan Can Be Recognized in Difficult Situations

Nevertheless, some of the difficult situations we encounter will be as a result of God's plan—a plan much greater than all the distress and the pain we can experience from the situation. Obviously Paul did not know that his situation was allowed by God. He only came to understand that God had allowed his situation to continue after he had engaged God in prayer—asking the Lord to take away the situation. We too may struggle to understand that some situations are allowed by God, until we engage the Lord in earnest prayer. It is through the inspiration of the Holy Spirit that we can come to understand this scripture and be encouraged by it in our times of difficulty.

It is true that the Bible both in the New Testament and Old

Testament—shows that Satan has no power other than that allowed him by God. [24] As stated in the previous section, Satan is an enemy who has *some* power to afflict our lives in with a variety of ways. No one is immune to the activities of evil forces. We should however understand that there are times that Satan will affect our lives when it is not part of God's plan—when our difficult situations are purely as a result of satanic influence, as covered in the previous section. It is in such situations where, if we prayed to the Lord for help, and actively denounce Satan, that we will see our situations change. This section is however focusing on situations that the Lord permits to occur in our lives. Because these situations are allowed by the Lord for some purpose, the situation will continue (until the time determined by God)—even after engaging the Lord in intense and persistent prayer. Looking at Pauls' situation (2 Corinthians 12:7 –10), it is clear that he expected the Lord would take the undesired situation away. He was, however, to learn that his situation presented him the opportunity to understand the Lord's purpose over his life in a significant way. As noted earlier, it was only after he engaged God about the situation through persistent prayer that he became aware that the situation was serving God's greater purpose in his life. The Lord allowed him to endure the situation in order to help him from becoming arrogant, because of the wealth of revelations that he had received from the Lord (vs 7). It seems the all-knowing God knew that Paul would have struggled to balance his spiritual experiences with the level of humility required. This struggle is not unique to Paul. It is a challenge for all humans—to be in a place of privilege, and at the same time be able to remain humble and overcome the temptation of pride. It appears the Lord had determined that Paul needed some kind of limitation to help him balance that. The thorn in the flesh seemingly served as a reminder for him that in spite of his great spiritual experiences—he

---

[24] Carson, A. Donald, France, T. Richard, Motyer J. Alec and Gordon J. Wenham. *New Bible Commentary*. Leicester: IVP, 1994.

remained an imperfect human—who has limitations like everyone else. That serves to highlight the distinction between humans and the sovereign Lord— who has no weakness or limit. Not only that, if Paul had become arrogant, his relationship with the Lord would have been seriously affected. All that he had gained through the experiences would become of less value. Proverbs 16:18 for instance highlights that "Pride goes before destruction, and a haughty spirit before a fall" (NIV). I surmise that after Paul understood this perspective, he considered it better to endure the will of God (the difficult situation), than to live outside of God's will.

Trusting God's Judgement

While God heard Paul's prayer, Paul's situation continued. Paul's response to this demonstrates that he trusted the Lord's judgement of his situation. First, it is important to note that he did not become angry at God for not taking the situation away. He was rather satisfied with God's response; "My grace is sufficient for you" (2 Corinthians 12:9 NIV). This phrase effectively means that in spite of Paul's negative experience, the Lord was involved in his life much more positively— more positive than merely taking away the thorn. Paul does not consider that the Lord had abandoned him. He was content with how the Lord was handling his situation. "God promised Paul that in the midst of the weakness and frustrations he would find God's power all the more present."[25] Therefore, instead of questioning God, he was mature enough to understand that whatever was happening to him, it was more advantageous that he endured it—as long as he was in the plan and will of God.

---

[25] Carson, A. Donald, France, T. Richard, Motyer J. Alec and Gordon J. Wenham. *New Bible Commentary*," p.1024.

The Key Lesson from Paul's Experience

What can we make out of Paul's experience of 2 Corinthians 12? We learn from Paul's encounter that we should expect that some difficult situations will continue— even when we have sought the Lord to remove them. This is not easy to accept. Nevertheless, there will be situations that the Lord will allow for a more beneficial purpose—a purpose that overshadows the ill-effects of the situation. There is a sense that when Paul understood that it was God's will for his situation to continue for a spiritual purpose, he chose to have the purpose overshadow his feelings about the situation. For our reassurance, when God allows situations to occur and persist, He will give us the comfort and understanding like Paul— that even if our immediate problem does not go away, we are safer than if we did not have that problem, and living a life that is out of God's plan. That would be a bigger problem! We can see that Paul continued to serve the Lord in ministry, even with this *thorn in the flesh*— whatever it was.

Basing on Paul's experience, we learn that the Lord may use different means to help us become the people that He has purposed us to be, individually. Everyone will have their own life path and destiny. We are all unique and different. Our experiences with God are different and unique. Our personalities, characters, weaknesses and strengths are also unique. The all-knowing God, however, knows what each one of us needs in order to be where He needs us to be in life, and spiritually. Sometimes He chooses to use and allow life situations that may be undesirable for us. We only need to remain faithful and committed to our relationship with Him. He will comfort and strengthen us supernaturally, like Paul—leading to the lessening of the burden of our challenges. While this is the case, the obvious problem we encounter in this is that we will not always know which of our situations are allowed by God. There is also a second problem that in embracing this view, we may consider that every difficult situation is part of God's plan: including situations inflicted on us by Satan—situations that actually require us to pray about, in order to make way for God's intervention. To address these two challenges, we do not need to look further. We need to look at how Paul came to understand that his situation was allowed by God: (1) we need to understand that Paul did not write this passage to the Corinthians (his audience) in real time. He is rather writing after a time of reflection. As a result, he had a better understanding of the situation at the point of writing, than when he first experienced the situation and (2) Paul had prayed about the situation asking the Lord to take it away (12:8). He would hardly have come to understand what God was doing through his situation, had he not taken time to consult or seek help from the Lord. It was through his dialogue with the Lord that he started to get God's perspective of his situation. It is only after engaging God about the situation that he learnt that the Lord knew about his situation, and that He was allowing it to continue—but for a greater cause. Therefore, while life throws a lot of challenges and difficulties at us, we may be able to identify which situations are allowed by God in our lives—if we take time to consult the Lord in times of difficulty like Paul. It is important that all situations are presented to the Lord in prayer (Philippians 4:6). As in Paul's case, this may mean persistent prayer. Prayer is not only there to enable us to understand God's insight, but it is also through prayer that we can receive divinely inspired comfort and peace in difficult situations, like Paul. It is the kind of peace and comfort that outshines all kinds of distress and pain. Apart from the more perfect example of Paul, I too have personally experienced this comfort and peace when the Lord was working in my life through one of the most challenging phases of my journey of life. I have dedicated the next chapter to that experience.

CHAPTER 9

A Road Marked with Suffering— A Personal Experience

I became involved in ministry leadership at the age of 22. Living in London, I became involved in various ministry areas, which included church planting and leadership. I emerged into the local and national leadership of a church denomination. I was fortunate to have the Holy Spirit reveal some of my ministry gifts early on in life. I got married at 25, and by this time, my call to ministry had a specific calling and directive from the Lord to undergo ministry training. I was at the time truly committed to and enjoying serving the Lord as a lay worker. I considered that formal ministry training was for people who wanted to become fulltime ministers, including pastors. Although I valued and respected the work of pastors, I did not consider myself to have the desire or calling to be a pastor. I had in fact known lay church leaders who effectively and faithfully served as much as (or more than) ordained pastors. I however had the mind that if the Lord desires me to serve in a pastoral capacity, then I would. It just was not my preference, or at least at the time.

The Call to Ministry

In the process of time, things changed. It became very clear that the Lord had called me into pastoral ministry. Now living in Northwood (London), I started to search for a Bible College. In reality I did not look very far. I only looked at one reputable theological school in the UK. This was purely for strategic reasons. It was very convenient for me to enroll at the then London Bible College, for two reasons: (1) it was located literally right behind our house. This meant there would be no travel expense bill to go to college and (2) my wife's (Fungai) work place, Mt Vernon Hospital, was also just across the road. We could see both the college and the hospital from the house, on opposite sides. In my mind, this was the most strategic institution for studying that would save us money.

Nevertheless, our church was in Slough, which was about 15 miles away. Round about this time, there was a great revival in our church. The church was growing, and most notably spiritually. There was a great outpouring of the Holy Spirit, and we were experiencing a 'mini Azusa Street experience' for about 2 years. Because there was no designated pastor, the church was led by a leadership team of lay workers from the time we planted it. Because of this growth, the demand on the leadership increased. Fungai and I decided to move closer to the church, to support this. This is how committed to ministry my wife and I were as a young couple. We consequently moved to Langley which was 10 miles away from Northwood, and just about 2 miles outside of Slough central. I was at this time working at Central Middlesex Hospital in London, which was some 15 miles away from our new home. I was at this time wrestling with the thought and plan to resign work, and to enroll at London Bible College in Northwood for the strategic reasons stated above. Since Fungai still worked in Northwood, I had planned that I would travel to Northwood with her on her way to work—she worked there all week except weekends. This would work for us, since classes would be between Monday and Friday at the college.

In the progression of time, Fungai and I continued serving God in the church. I was at the same time promoted at work in my nursing job. This gave me some motivation in terms of employment. By way of career development, I enrolled for a part-time Degree in Health Promotion. At this time, the thought of enrolling for theological studies started to drift away. To cut a long story short, while I was starting to lose momentum on my plans to enroll into Bible College, the call to go into ministry training became intense and more urgent. I then started the process of applying for enrolment at London Bible College. After starting the application process, one night I got a clear vision showing that London Bible College was not the place I was to study. It was a message I got loud and clear. I had no doubt that this was the Lord guiding me to what He had specifically planned for me. In obedience I started searching again for theological training institutions. My search was more widened, and this time incorporated much prayer. I was subsequently led to go to Mattersey Hall, the Assemblies of God official Bible College in Retford, Yorkshire, in the North East of England. With all that was happening, I discontinued my Health Promotion Degree studies, and enrolled for a foundational Certificate in Biblical Studies at Mattersey Hall. I completed this in about a year, through distance learning. After completing the certificate level, I applied to pursue my undergraduate studies full-time. It is at this time that we relocated to the North East. With much prayer along the way, the Lord gave us a green light to proceed with this plan. I personally had many visions showing how I would experience challenges ahead of me. It was a matter of the Lord stating that while He was directing me to follow this direction, it was not going to be smooth sailing. Both Fungai and I were very sure we were following God's leading on this. We moreover made some practical actions to support the plan. The first thing we did was to secure jobs in the area where we would be moving to. We both were accepted and offered positions in different healthcare organizations. This was around April 2005. My aim was to work full-time in this position up to the time that I started full-time studies. This would have enabled me to pay for at least my first year tuition fees in advance. Fungai would continue to work full-time after I started college in the month of September. All was in place—based on our planning.

Soon after moving to Doncaster near Retford things did not work out as we had planned. My job offer was withdrawn just before I had even started. At the same time Fungai sustained an injury at work. She was unable to work a long time after that. Because she was a new employee in the organization, she had very limited sick pay and had to leave that employment. This resulted in us both being unemployed. Our savings dwindled and subsequently ran out. It was a very difficult situation financially, and this impacted on our lives as a family. Our son Enoch was a year old. This moreover impacted on my tuition fees for Bible College. I was convinced that my nursing profession would help me to resolve the situation quickly. I made many applications for work. When I could not get anything in nursing, I started applying for any kind of job, with no success. I could not get a job in spite of constantly making numerous applications. Even when I registered with employment agencies for non-professional jobs—I was never offered a job. Not even a shift. Many people I know who registered with the same agencies together with me, or after, where offered opportunities to work. Some started working only days after they registered. Over the months, I regularly made calls to and visited the agencies to track the progress and to almost beg for a job. I still could not get a job. Life suddenly changed—from a life where I could afford anything I wanted, to a life where I could not afford the basics. This life was characterized by growing debt, humiliation from a number of experiences and a sense of helplessness in regards to supporting my wife and child. It felt like all doors had closed on us. It felt like I was in a *dark tunnel* of life. The simple and natural straightforward opportunities and processes seemed impossible for us. I perceived that this was not a normal experience. I concluded that Satan was battling us in a big way.

I nonetheless remained steadfast in my trust and hope in

the Lord. I never gave up or abandoned my faith or service for Christ. In fact, this is the time I prayed the most in my life. I would spend much time in prayer, which was regularly accompanied by fasting—mainly for my wife's healing, but also as a means of actively denouncing Satan's influence in our situation. In this time, I experienced exponential growth in my faith and relationship with Christ. I would wake up and go upstairs into the spare bedroom, lie on my back facing the ceiling, and talk to God for an hour or two—each time. I did this every day, and sometimes more than once in a day. I carried on serving the Lord faithfully in the local church, which we had become part of—as part of the leadership team. Fungai served in the women's ministry leadership. God was using us both to help many others through His Spirit. We were seeing the supernatural intervention of God in the lives of the people we ministered to and supported. The paradox is however that while we saw God work in the lives of others, we could not say that we were seeing God working particularly in my Fungi's health, our work situation and finances. The financial situation was getting worse. Our situation generated many views and perceptions. In the eyes of others, we had made the wrong move to leave London. To others we were a zealous young couple who had a genuine call of God on their lives—who had nevertheless hastily pursued the call with no real plan. To others we had done something very bad that God was punishing us for. In my view, however, none of these perceptions really affected me. Fungai and I were more than 100% sure that we had responded to the Lord's call, and that the time we left London was right and was God-led.

The Lord was to do something that proved to show that he was with us in the situation. It had become clear that I was not able to start Bible College that September, as I had missed the deadline for paying my tuition fees. The college had communicated to this effect, and classes were moreover due to start in the following few weeks. Nevertheless, about 2 weeks before the college opened, they contacted me again—this time informing me that I could start that September, because an anonymous sponsor had paid part of my tuition fees. I couldn't believe this. This was a miracle! My *dark tunnel* was suddenly lit. Although this did not instantaneously resolve all our challenges, it came to me as a sign to show that the Lord was not distant from our situation, as it had seemed at times. I have learnt from this and other situations that; in the midst of situations, the Lord will act in some positive way as a message to say, "I am with you".

I am reminded of Joseph's story in the Bible. God's hand was visible in Joseph's life even though he lived in captivity in Egypt. Young Joseph was sold into slavery by his brothers (Genesis 37:12 –36). He was unwillingly taken to a strange country; away from his family and everything he knew. This was an extremely challenging situation for someone who is understood to have only been a teenager at the time. In the face of this challenge, it is clear that the Lord was with him, while he was a servant in Potiphar's household. "Potiphar noticed this and realized that the Lord was with Josep*h*" (39:3 NIV) and he in no time "made Joseph his personal attendant" (39:4 NIV), and further "put him in charge of his entire household and everything he owned" (39:4b NIV). Nevertheless, after turning down Potiphar's wife's request to sleep with her, she responded by falsely accusing Joseph for attempting to rape her—leading to his imprisonment (vs 6-18). In spite of all this gloom and doom around him, the Lord was to yet again demonstrate to Joseph that He was with him. In no time after landing in prison "the warden put Joseph in charge of all the other prisoners and over everything that happened in the prison" (39:23 NLT). Joseph however continued in prison until he was released to become second in command to the Egyptian King, at the age of 30 (41:6).

Like Joseph, even after seeing God's hand in our situation, the situation continued through my years in Bible College. Fungi's health was getting better but she remained out of work for much of my college life. Nonetheless, in all that, Fungai and I became so close. We learnt to trust in God for the next meal, with little anxiety. We continued in prayer about our whole situation. Our prayers included fasting and combating any of Satan's influence and power that may have influenced our situation. After many months of prayer, we had come to the understanding that through persistent faith and prayers, Satan would by this point in time have been defeated, if at all he was the source of our situation. In time, I started to sense more and more that Satan was not in control of our situation. While I consider it very likely that Satan was the agent of our bad experiences as in Job's case (Job Chapter 1), I was more convinced and reassured that it was God who was in control. I came to a place of peace and calmness in my life that I had never been before, even though I was enduring unprecedented life challenges. I eventually got to a point that I was no longer praying for the situation. I was sure that the Lord had heard all our prayers, and that He was allowing the situation to continue for some reason. God was doing something in our lives. We were being prepared in many ways; in areas such as humility, patience, hope, perseverance, and total dependence on God. I grew to understand more of what Paul was teaching to the Christian community at Philippi when he wrote, "I know what it is to be in need, and I know what it is to have plenty. I have learned the secret of being content in any and every situation, whether well fed or hungry, whether living in plenty or in want" (Philippians 4:12 NIV). However, Fungai's health was restored. She was able to work again. When our situation started to become better, we realized that both Fungai and I had learnt a great deal about life, and about God. Looking back, although the whole experience was unpleasant, it strengthened my faith, personal walk with Christ and ministry. The situation taught me to empathize more with people going through difficult situations when ministering to them. The overall lesson for me through this lengthy experience was the fact that the Lord can allow some undesired and unpleasant experiences (whether caused by Satan or not) to occur to—us in order to bring the best out of us. On reflection, I actually appreciate the Lord for allowing me to go through this lesson, and particularly to go through it with Him.

CHAPTER 10

Looking Forward to What Lies Ahead

In a previous chapter, I highlighted the fact that various factors influence and or cause difficult situations to occur in life. Because every situation is unique, it is important to take time to particularly seek to understand if a situation you find yourself in is a consequence of a wrong choice, decision/action or otherwise. I appreciate we are not always certain of this. It is however possible to identify some of the situations that arise as a direct result of our choices, decisions and actions. In that case, we should not lose heart. Making wrong decisions, choices and actions is not the end of the world. We all do at some point in life, and later on regret ever making them. The key is, however, to remain positive about the future and not dwell on what has already been done. Paul shares one of his life principles on this. He says that he forgets the things of the past and stretches forward to what is ahead (Philippians 3:13). What are these past experiences that he chooses to forget?, we may ask. The Bible however does not elaborate. To understand the meaning of Paul's statement in Philippians 3:13 in greater depth, we need to explore some possibilities of what he was referring to. This will enable us to understand the principle of looking ahead to a hopeful future— instead of dwelling on past experiences.

Here are a few possibilities of what Paul was referring to. First, this may be pointing to the pleasant experiences in his relationship with, and service for Christ. We are sure that Paul had some wonderful experiences in God. 2 Corinthians 12 is an example of a phenomenal experience of Paul in the Lord. Who would not want to reminisce or even boast about such an experience? We all do have some pleasant experiences that we do reminisce about. That is not wrong. It is actually healthy to do that. If this is what he is referring to, then the point he is making is that although he has had pleasant experiences in Christ, he will not allow those past experiences to cloud him, and cause him to lose focus on the present and future experiences with God. This is a good principle—as long as we do not let such experiences hinder us from progressing forward. We should be determined to have more experiences God, not only in our past lives, but in the present and the future. Secondly, the Bible reveals how he (in his former life as Saul) persecuted the church of God (Acts 8:1– 8). If this is the past he was referring to, Paul would be stating that he will look ahead, and not dwell on his past failures. Thirdly, the past may be referring to his experiences of his sufferings for the sake of the kingdom. If we consider this, Paul may well be acknowledging that while he had gone through some difficulties in his life he was determined to look beyond them, and look to brighter experiences of life ahead.

Lastly, let's consider the immediate context of the preceding verse (Philippians 3:12). Paul says of himself that he has not yet achieved his goal—and so he presses on. He openly reveals that he has not achieved perfection. He might be referring to the fact that he acknowledges his shortcomings. Looking at all these possibilities, we can come to an understanding of the experiences Paul choses to look beyond in Philippians 3:13. So whether it is his past pleasant experiences, bad past experiences, his sufferings through persecution, his weaknesses and failures or all of these put together; Paul in this text highlights a good principle. The principle of consciously choosing not to be bound by the past, but to focus on the future.

The heart of this principle is that he is determined not to allow past experiences be a hindrance over his future. Many people will benefit from this wonderful Godly principle. It may not be easy to progress from past experiences. Experiences are very powerful. In my pastoral ministry experience, I have had many encounters of believers presenting to me with feelings of failure that arise from making bad decisions in their past. Some are affected by their past so severely that they may fail to progress, even spiritually. God however wants us to let go of negative past experiences, so that we can look ahead to a brighter future.

Isaiah's prophecy to Israel begins by uttering God's sharp disapproval of their evil ways. In the later part of Isaiah's prophecy, the merciful God our Father, assures them of restoration: "forget the former things; do not dwell on the past. See I am doing a new thing!" (Isaiah 43:18 – 19 NIV). This passage is considered by many Bible scholars to be reflective of the key theme of the entire book of Isiah[26]. In view of this scripture, the Bible is not teaching that we erase our memories of the past. NO! There are many past life experiences, both positive and negative, that when reflected upon—can impact our present and future in a positive way. While past experiences can help us to improve our present and future— they can on the other hand potentially be harmful. The context of both Paul's principle and God's Word spoken by the Prophet Isaiah (43:18 –19), however, encourages us to look to a brighter future and not dwell on the past. This is also the key message of this chapter. As an example, Apostle Paul had many challenging experiences. He had been through "great endurance; troubles, hardships and distresses; beatings, imprisonments and riots; hard work, sleepless nights and hunger...." (2 Corinthians 6:4 –5 NIV). He however chose not to dwell on these experiences, but chose to focus on the positive goals of his life and ministry.

In the case of Israel, God was calling them out of their existing

---

[26] Brueggeman, Walter. *Isaiah 1 – 39*. Kentucky: Westminister Knox, 1998.

situation—into a brighter future. He said to them, "Come now, let us settle the matter," 'says the Lord'. "Though your sins are like scarlet, they shall be as white as snow; though they are red as crimson, they shall be like wool (Isaiah 1:18 NIV). The nation of Israel had made the foolish decision to turn away from God. This left them vulnerable and open to the world's hostilities. Other nations became militarily stronger than them. In spite of their sin and foolishness, God was willing to give them a fresh start— if they turned back to Him.

Similarly, Jesus says, "Come to me, all you who are weary and burdened, and I will give you rest"(Matthew 11:28 NIV). He offers us rest from any kind of situation: this includes the situations that we bring upon ourselves through our actions, and those that Satan throws at us. We only need to accept Jesus' invitation, and take our burdens to the Lord in prayer, believing that He will give us rest. The pains and disappointments of life can cause us to lose hope, particularly when a situation continues for a long time. We should however be inspired by the likes of Job and Joseph. They serve as examples to show that when we continue to trust God, He will help us. Our faith is demonstrated and made stronger when we continue to trust God in difficult times. Shadrach, Meshach and Abednego displayed this quality when they were forced to denounce God by worshiping an idol or face the fate of a fiery furnace. They displayed faith at its best: (1) they declared their belief that God had the power to deliver them and (2) they declared that they would not abandon God, even if they were to die in the fire (Daniel 3:18). This is a high level of maturity: knowing that the love and honor for God is based on who He is to us, and not on Him always doing what we want Him to do for us.

Nevertheless, it is important to remain positive even if a situation persists. A positive mind is a breeding ground for faith, but a negative mind is a breeding ground for doubt. God however responds positively to faith (when we trust His ability to help us). He on the other hand despises a doubting heart, as demonstrated in Matthew 14:31. All barriers to faith that include sin, anxieties and doubt should be addressed by prayer. Faith is a key to answered prayer. It is also important for Christians to understand that answered prayer is more than the vanishing of the situation. When a situation persists, it is common for people to consider that God has not answered their prayer. I used to have that kind of thinking. I have had instances where it took me a long time to realize that God had answered my prayers. This is because I was primarily concerned with an instant change and the removal of the situation's symptoms, rather than taking time to learn what God was doing.

When my brother was diagnosed of cancer in 2000, after much prayer, the Lord revealed that He had restored his life. However, after receiving that revelation, his health actually took a downturn. It took at least another year from that time to realize his total healing and restoration (physically, psychologically, emotionally & financially). The Lord fulfilled His Word. While medical experts expected Heath to live only a few months after his diagnosis, he is still alive today and cancer free—17 years on. It was a lesson on the fact that God answers prayer, and that healing and restoration is not always instant: it can be a process. The same is true for Job, Joseph and probably many that read this book. So don't give up! God may have answered your prayers already, and you may just be going through the process of restoration.

Having learnt that Satan's attack on our lives is real (1Peter 5:8), we should continue to pray for the Lord to intervene in our situations. This should include directly countering Satan's activity in our lives, just as Jesus did in the lives of many. This may include prayers that include fasting. Jesus taught us that we are better equipped to overcome some kinds of satanic activities by prayer and fasting. Jesus explained this after healing a young boy whose inability to speak and hear was caused by an evil spirit. After Jesus commanded the spirit to leave the boy, the disciples consulted Jesus and asked why they themselves had failed in their attempt to deliver the young boy (Mark 9:28). His response was: "This kind can come out by nothing but prayer and fasting" (vs.29 NKJV). Seeing that prayer is such an important aspect of how we respond to life challenges, the subjects of prayer (and fasting) are discussed in the following two chapters.

CHAPTER 11

Insights into Prayer

In previous chapters, I explained the importance and effect of prayer when dealing with or responding to life difficult situations. This chapter will focus on prayer. Prayer is more of an act (practical) than it is theory. No amount of theory alone will fully explain prayer. The essence of prayer has to be experienced at an individual level. Therefore, any amount of theory or theology of prayer will at best provide some guidance and a framework for experiencing or putting prayer into action. This will present some valuable insights on understanding prayer more effectively; particularly in the face of challenges.

I expect that many people who choose to read a book of this genre will be Christians who already have some understanding and application of prayer in their lives. Prayer is something that Christians do with little or no thought. It is part of the faith and practice of Christianity. Christian faith is, however, a journey of continuous learning. Many Christians have found the insights in this chapter uplifting. I am therefore hopeful that many more will find this chapter helpful, one way or the other.

'Relationship' - is at the Heart of Prayer

Prayer, like Christianity, is largely relational. It is not some sort of 'magical' formula, 'chant' or 'get-out of jail card' that is pulled out and used in a moment of need, as in the board game, monopoly. There are two key players in the practice of prayer: (1) a person or people who are praying and (2) One who is prayed to— God (Jehovah). The Bible is clear on the fact t that God the Creator of all things (Genesis 1:1; Nehemiah 9:6; Revelations 4:11) is not a natural being. He cannot be seen (John 1:18; 1 Timothy 1:17) or accessed in the natural. "God is a Spirit" (John 4:25 KJV). This means that the Godhead (the manifestation of God in the form of Father, Spirit and Son) is supernatural (beyond the natural realm) as elaborated in 1 John 5:7 – 8. He exists in a realm that is beyond the natural realm of humans and nature. In other words, while God can, and does manifest in the natural realm, His existence transcends the natural realm, which is His creation. This is a very fundamental point that has to be understood, which is pertinent to prayer.

Humans Have a Special Place in God's Heart

The Bible gives us a hint of the relationship that God purposed between Him and humans. From His intimate relationship with the first human, Adam, we can observe that God's intention is to relate and interact with humans (Genesis 3: 8 –11; Acts 17: 26 –27). God moreover gave humans a special place amongst all that He created. The nature of humans and their relationship with God is comes out more clearly in what is often referred to as the doctrine or theme of 'the image of God in man'. The creation of humans was unique. Unlike the creation of all other things, when creating humans, God distinctively commanded, "Let us make mankind in our image, in our likeness…" (Genesis 1:26 NIV). "So God created mankind in his own image, in the image of God he created them; male and female he created them" (vs 27 NIV). We do not fully understand and cannot precisely explain the exact details of the likeness. However, the Bible points to the fact that humans are "in some way and some degree like God."[27] We should of course not see humans as identical or equal to the Sovereign God. We can, however, understand the image of God in man by identifying the part of human which man shares with God. Throughout the history of biblical interpretation there has been a consistent understanding that humans have a spirit aspect, and that this is one important aspect that humans share with God.[28] On one hand we have God, who is spirit; on the other hand we have humans, who while physical beings, have a spirit element. Therefore, when we enter into relationship with God (when we become saved), our spirit part converges with God (who is Spirit) through the channel of the Holy Spirit (God's Spirit). Our communication with God is therefore a spiritual act. On this, the Bible explains that those who seek to worship (or pray to) Him, should do so in a mode that is not natural, but rather "...worship Him in the spirit..." (John 4:25 NIV). In summary, communication between God and people is a spiritual process that is facilitated by the Holy Spirit. The Holy Spirit links the spirit part of the person to God (who is Spirit).

What Do We Pray?

Because prayer is relational, it is an expression or communication of thoughts and feelings from a person (or group of people) towards God. This is internally carried out in the heart and mind, and often expressed verbally (externally). Prayer is therefore largely individualistic, as it is an expression of thoughts and feelings. One good example of prayer in the Bible that illustrates this perspective is that of Hannah—when she sought God's attention concerning her

---

[27] Clines, D.J.A. "Tyndale Old Testament lecture, 1967: The Image of God in Man." *Tyndale Bulletin* 19 (1968): 53

[28] Clines, "Tyndale Old Testament lecture, 1967: The Image of God in Man."

inability to conceive (1 Samuel 1:12 –20). Apart from her deep desire to conceive a child, there were other aspects of her situation described in the text, which made her situation even more burdensome. She consequently took it upon herself to speak to God and to passionately seek His attention and intervention in her situation. God heard her, and enabled her to conceive and give birth to a son. From this and other examples, we can see that prayer is an expression of what is within an individual's heart. While in this chapter I approach prayer in the context of facing difficult situations, prayer is a means of communicating with God at all times.

Prayer is More Effective When We are Close to God

To help explain how our relationship with God motivates and strengthens prayer, I will draw a practical life example. When in need of help we usually turn to those closest to us such as family and close friends, rather than strangers. It is the established close relationship that gives us the cause, motivation and comfort to seek and ask help from those close to us. Likewise, those who have an established personal relationship with God, will find cause, motivation and comfort in seeking help and guidance from God— in times of difficulty. This does not mean that those who are new to Christianity should refrain from calling on Him in times of difficulty. No. God is gracious and hears His people. In fact, some people soon after becoming a Christian; have prayed for the first time, asking God's help in times of difficulty—and He answered their prayers. God answers prayer even when people are new to Christianity, or when they pray for the first time. The Bible, however, highlights that the prayer of a "righteous" person is powerful and effective (James 5:16b). Because it is Christ Who makes us right with God—"righteousness" here can be understood as having a more intimate relationship with Christ.

How Should We Pray?

The best available resource on the essence of prayer and how believers should pray is the Lord Jesus Christ. In Matthew 6:9 –13, He presented His followers with some guidance on prayer—in what has been labelled the 'Lord's Prayer' throughout generations:

> Our Father in heaven,
> Hallowed be your name,
> Your kingdom come,
> Your will be done,
> On earth as it is in heaven,
> Give us today our daily bread,
> And forgive us our debts,
> As we also have forgiven our debtors,
> And lead us not into temptation,
> but deliver us from the evil one…(NIV)

Many people the world over, both Christians and non-Christians alike, have recited this prayer, traditionally. However, the prayer is worth more than tradition and what is perceived at face value. It is the most explicit guidance on how to pray offered in the Bible. There has been the question of whether the prayer should be prayed verbatim. The essence of the prayer is however of more value than the question of whether or not we should pray it word for word. It is important to highlight here that Jesus is teaching beyond the lyrics of a prayer. Rather, He is teaching the attitude in which we should approach our Good Father (God), in prayer.

1. Submitting to God's Sovereignty

Firstly, the prayer highlights the importance of acknowledging the sovereignty of God. The opening line of the prayer, **Our Father in Heaven,** upholds the importance and necessity of affirming and confirming one's identification with God. Every occasion of prayer is an opportunity for God's children to acknowledge, express and celebrate the Father's (God) sovereignty. This attitude is beneficial to the one who is praying. It inspires the confidence and reassurance that in prayer, you are approaching God the Father and Creator of all things. This also brings you to a place of submitting towards the will of the Father. This opens the invitation to God and demonstrates your willingness for Him to be involved your life or situation.

2. Presenting Our Needs to God

Second, the line *Give us today our daily bread* underlines the fact that God provides for His people. God has revealed Himself to mankind as *Jehovah-Jireh*, which means, The Lord Who will see to our needs (The Lord Who provides) (Genesis 22:12 –14). Matthew 6:25-33 describes the nature of God as a provider more clearly. Jesus explains that it is God who provides: (1) food for the wild birds—since they do not plant, harvest or produce food for themselves and (2) natural covering for the flowers, grass and plants. The key message in that passage highlights the fact that if God can provide for nature (i.e. wild animals and vegetation), He is even more able and willing to provide for humans. It underlines the very fact that just being alive is a sure sign that God has allowed you to live (6:25). So while we may experience need, the fact that we are here is the evidence of God providing life. Of course just being alive is not enough—as life presents us with needs or challenges. The Bible therefore directs us to depend on God for provision. The prayer model presented by Jesus to His disciples, above, teaches that our prayers should include asking God for provision, which is depicted by the example of asking God for daily food (i.e. daily bread). God's provision will come in a variety of ways. It does not entail that God will necessarily and literally bring food to someone's table. God will however provide opportunities and channels for provision. This may include opportunities for paid work etc. The Bible in Philippians 4:6 guides us on how to respond when faced with situations that cause us to worry about any aspect of life: "… pray about everything. Tell God what you need, and thank him for all he has done" (NLT). Beyond the practical provision, we should also expect to "…experience God's peace, which exceeds anything we can understand. His peace will guard your hearts and minds as you live in Christ Jesus" (vs7 NLT).

3. Sin Affects the Effectiveness of Prayer

Third, the Bible is clear that God despises sin (wrong doing) and disobedience. Sin therefore significantly affects the effectiveness of prayer: "Listen! The Lord's arm is not too weak to save you, nor is his ear too deaf to hear you call. It's your sins that have cut you off from God. Because of your sins, he has turned away and will not listen anymore" (Isaiah 59:1–2 NLT). When we acknowledge and accept Jesus as our Savior—God forgives all our sin, and removes the punishment of permanent death (Romans 6:23), and the eternal suffering of the soul, beyond death (Matthew 25:46; 2 Thessalonians 1:9; Revelations 21:8), which sin deserves. We are, however, instructed not to take God's grace for granted, by continuing to live in sin. Instead, we are instructed to do away with sin (Hebrews 12:1; Timothy 2:22). There are two key ways of dealing with sin: (1) to avoid sinning and (2) to confess sin once it has been committed. So while we should be determined to avoid sin at all costs, we will at some point find ourselves having done the very thing that we despise—sin against our God. In order to continually enjoy the forgiveness of sin that Jesus has made available for us, we should confess our sins, asking **God to forgive us our sin**— as directed in the Lord's Prayer. By confessing our sin, we continually disassociate ourselves with the sinful nature of our humanity, and align ourselves with God's righteousness. "People who conceal their sins will not prosper, but if they confess and turn from them, they will receive mercy" (Proverbs 28:13 NLT). God's mercy on us was fulfilled by Jesus on the Cross. We, however, uphold the mercy we received by continually demonstrating our distaste of sin—because we sometimes find ourselves in the trap of sin. "If we claim we have no sin, we are only fooling ourselves and not living in the truth. But if we confess our sins to him, he is faithful and just to forgive us our sins and to cleanse us from all wickedness" (1 John 1:7 – 9 NLT). Therefore, prayer gives us the opportunity to eliminate sin and guilt. This will cause our relationship and communication with God to flourish. Here are examples of key biblical figures who incorporated repentance: (1) Moses in Exodus 32:31– 32, (2) Ezra in Chapter 9:6 –15 of his book and (3) Daniel in Chapter 9:4 –19 of his book.

4. Lead Us Not Into Temptation

The fourth element of the Lord's Prayer (temptation to sin) is closely linked to the previous (asking for forgiveness of sin). The previous section highlighted how God reviles sin, and how sin affects our relationship and communication with God. This section emphasises the need for us to disassociate from sin continually. However, humans: (1) are naturally susceptible to temptation to sin (Genesis 6:5; Genesis 8:2; James 1 13 –14; 1 Thessalonians 3:5) and (2) need supernatural help (Holy Spirit) to overcome temptation, which in other circumstances may be influenced by Satan's (supernatural) powers/activity (Matthew 4:1-11). Christ, as One Who did not yield to temptation, in the Lord's Prayer advises His disciples to pray and ask for God's help to overcome temptation. There is a constant conflict of desires between our flesh and the spirit (Galatians 5:17; Romans 7:14 – 24). It is through prayer that we conquer temptation. If we allow the spirit of God to lead our lives, we will become closer to God in our relationship as 'God's Children' (Romans 8:14).

5. Deliver Us From Evil

The fifth element alludes to the existence of the evil spiritual world that has the potential to affect the natural world and its inhabitants including Christians (Ephesians 6:12–20). Some believe that Christians should not be concerned or conscious of the existence and effect of Satan on their lives. This element on prayer reiterates, as discussed in chapter 8, that Satan is constantly seeking means and ways to 'attack' humanity (Revelations 12:12)—including believers. This is demonstrated by the number of references to spiritual conflict or warfare in the Bible. The message of the New Testament (NT), in particular, is aimed at those who are in Christ (believers). It, therefore, means that the sections of the NT, which highlight Satan as a threat to mankind, are too, directed to believers. Jesus hence teaches us to use prayer as a means to combat Satan's evil forces. Believers should pray and ask God the Father to help them fight against evil forces (***deliver us from evil***). This is consistent with the guidance in Ephesian 6, which shows that prayer is a means of overcoming satanic powers. "…pray in the Spirit on all occasions with all kinds of prayers and requests" (vs 8 NIV). Believers should, however, be aware and encouraged that they have been spiritually equipped to overcome satanic powers. Prayer is the means by which we can access the spiritual realm in order to confront situations that are influenced by evil spirits.

Summary

In summary, prayer is not necessarily telling God or informing God about your plight, as if He were not aware of our situations. God knows everything. Prayer is a vehicle for: (1) expressing worship to God the Father, (2) requesting the provision of daily needs, (3) continually disassociating with sin, (4) requesting supernatural help to overcoming temptation and (5) requesting for supernatural help to combat the activity and influence of Satan.

CHAPTER 12

Insights on Fasting (Prayer that is associated with fasting)

The Bible encourages believers to pray in the spirit with all kinds of prayers and requests (Ephesians 6:18). There are indeed different kinds of prayers that are appropriate for responding to different situations. To make this point, I will start by drawing an example from Hannah; the woman in 1 Samuel who could not have children. She was further ridiculed for her bareness by Peninnah, her husband's other wife who had children. It was common to have more than one wife in their culture and day. However, having children was expected of every married woman, and failure to have children was dishonorable. As a result, those who were unable to have children felt and lived in shame (see Luke 1:25). Peninnah added to Hannah's misery by mocking her for her situation. This situation spanned years (1:7). It is one thing to be in a pressing situation, and this made it even more difficult for her. She however responded to her distressing situation by prayer. In her distress she went to God and prayed—asking if God would give her a child. Hannah believed in God and prayed to specifically ask for a son. Having a son was more desirable in their culture. A son would carry the family name, and was therefore positioned to expand the family. Hannah's prayer was unique. It involved abstaining from food (I Samuel 1:7–8). She prayed to the Lord in what the Bible describes as 'deep anguish', and 'weeping bitterly' (1 Samuel 1:10; 1:16). Her abstaining from food as she prayed to God can be linked with prayer that is associated with abstaining from food, which is understood from a Christian perspective as 'fasting' (i.e. abstaining from physical nourishment). Fasting is a form of intense prayer that can be applied in different situations, including responding to difficult situations.

Basic Understanding of Fasting

The idea of fasting is not new to many people, and is not restricted to Christianity or to prayer. Fasting in the general sense is the act of abstaining from some or all food, drink or both for a period of time. In the medical context, people may be asked to fast under medical observation for investigation of medical problem(s). Patients undergoing an operation under general anesthetic are usually provided with information about fasting before an operation—explaining they are not allowed to eat or drink because of how anesthetic works. Anesthetic temporarily stops body reflexes. The presence of food and drink therefore presents a risk of vomiting, or bringing up food into the throat. This food can further spill into the lungs, and affect breathing or cause damage to the lungs. The general meaning of fasting is therefore universal.

Biblical Fasting

By considering Hannah's example above, abstaining from food for the purposes of prayer has a distinct purpose—different from the purpose of fasting for medical reasons. In biblical language, fasting is usually defined as a withholding of all natural food from the body for a determined period voluntarily appointed for moral or religious purposes. The Hebrew word for fast that is common in the Bible is *tsuwm*[29] (to cover the mouth)—which suggest no food or drink.[30] The Greek root word for fasting that is common in the Bible (New Testament) is *nesteuo*—which means to abstain from food and drink for religious purpose."[31] The Jewish encyclopedia describes fasting as "… a withholding of all natural food from the body for a determined period voluntarily appointed for moral or religious ends."[32] In view of this, fasting should be a voluntary spiritual discipline of abstaining from food, for the purposes of setting time aside (consecration) for greater focus on the Lord. Let's turn to some Bible examples where fasting was employed to respond to challenging situations.

Ezra's Fasting Experience

Ezra offers a biblical example of fasting in response to a difficult situation. Ezra had the important responsibility of leading two groups of Jews from a period of captivity in Babylon, back to their homeland. On his return with the second group, he was concerned for their safety due to possible attacks by enemies along the way. As a result, Ezra led the people to fast in order to seek God's protection: "Then I proclaimed a fast there, at the river Ahava, that we might deny ourselves before our God, to seek from him a safe journey for

[29] Bible Tools, "Strong's Hebrew Definition on Tsuwm." Accessed September 30, 2017. https://www.bibletools.org/index.cfm/fuseaction/Lexicon.show/ID/H6684/tsuwm.htm.

[30] Goldmon, Moses. *Choosing God's Fast: Biblical Strategies for Conquering Life's Challenges*. USA: Neumann Enterprises Publishing, 2012.

[31] Bible Tools, "New Testament Greek Lexicon Definition on Nesteuo." Accessed September 30, 2017. https://www.bibletools.org/index.cfm/fuseaction/Lexicons/greek/nas/nesteuo.html.

[32] Greenstone, H.Julius, Hirsch, G. Emil, Hirschfeld, Hartwig, "Fasting and Fast Days" in Jewish Encyclopedia: The unedited full-text of the 1906 Jewish Encyclopedia", 1906, accessed February 21, 2017. http://jewishencyclopedia.com/articles/6033-fasting-and-fast-days.

ourselves, our children, and all our possessions" (Ezra 8:21, NRSV). God answered them! "So we fasted and petitioned our God for this, and he listened to our entreaty" (vs 23 NRSV). "Then we left the river Ahava on the twelfth day of the first month, to go to Jerusalem; the hand of our God was upon us, and he delivered us from the hand of the enemy and from ambushes along the way" (vs31 NRSV). This text explains clearly the purpose of their fast, and the favorable results of their fasting.

Esther's Fasting Experience

The book of Esther provides a more explicit example of biblical fasting. Esther was a Jewish orphan and foreigner who later became a Queen—wife to king Ahasuerus. In the progression of time, Haman one of the king's officials had a feud with Mordecai, another Jewish (foreign) official—a cousin to Esther. In summary, the feud resulted in Haman coming up with a plan to influence the King to exterminate all Jews in his kingdom. Esther became concerned and distressed after she became aware of this, because she was also a Jew. In response, she rallied all the Jews to join her to seek the attention and intervention of God, through fasting. `She compelled them, "…Do not eat or drink for three days, night and day. I and my attendants will fast as you do. When this is done, I will go to the king, even though it is against the law. And if I perish, I perish" (Esther 4:16 NIV). Esther and the Jews followed through with their plan to fast (not eat or drink) for 3 days and nights, seeking God's supernatural intervention in their situation. Three unique things came out of their action as God responded favorably: (1) Esther got audience with the king, (2) the King miraculously overturned Haman's evil plan that was intended to annihilate the Jews. Instead, the King ordered Haman killed and (3) the king moreover ordered for the protection of the Jews for generations. The Jews thereafter assumed a special status, and became even more powerful (Esther chapters 5 –10).

Daniel's Fasting Experience

Daniel was a great intercessor. He was dedicated to praying for his nation. Therefore, after understanding that the nation was going into desolation, as a consequence of their wickedness, he prayed and pleaded with God with fasting. He says of this, "Then I turned to the Lord God, to seek an answer by prayer and supplication with fasting and sackcloth and ashes" (Daniel 9:3 NRSV). While Daniel has incorporated other kinds of prayer and devotion, Daniel specifically explains that he was fasting here (unlike his experiences of chapters 1:1-18 and 10:3—which will be discussed later). Nevertheless, God responded to Daniel's prayer and fasting, and He sent a messenger with a message to Daniel (Daniel 9: 21– 27).

Taking Hannah, Ezra, Esther and Daniel's examples above, we can see that abstaining from food was part of an expression for seeking and hoping for God's blessings (positive intervention) in a situation. The Bible presents a variety of reasons for fasting. The Jewish Virtual Library is a good resource in particularly demonstrating this point:

> The purposes of fasting are various. Its most widely attested function, for the community as well as the individual, is to avert or terminate a calamity by eliciting God's compassion. For example, God mitigates Ahab's punishment because he fasted and humbled himself (I Kings 21:27–29). ...Many other passages also indicate the use of fasting as a means of winning divine forgiveness (e.g., Ps. 35:13; 69:11; Ezra 10:6), implying that fasting is basically an act of penance, a ritual expression of remorse, submission, and supplication.[33]

[33] Jewish Virtual Library. "Fasting and Fast Days." Accessed July 29, 2017. https//:www.jewishvirtuallibrary.org/fasting-and-fast-days.

While this book primarily focuses on the aspect of how believers can respond to challenging situations, fasting is not restricted to such situations. For example, there is no indication that the church at Antioch (in Acts 13:1–3) was fasting in response to a difficult situation as seen in the other examples discussed above. The Acts 13:1–3 prayer and fast comes across as more devotional and possibly for seeking God's guidance for ministry. God responded to their prayer by giving them specific directions on ministry gifting and service. Fasting is therefore used as a form of prayer for different purposes. These will include seeking spiritual refreshing, strengthening of faith, seeking Divine guidance or wisdom, combating satanic influences and powers, or any desire for God's positive intervention in an individual or corporate (i.e. family /church/community etc.) life or situation. Fasting is a commitment and sacrifice of *humbling* one's self before the Lord to express heartfelt deep desires to the Lord (1 Peter 5:6) (James 4:10) (see 2 Samuel 12:16-18). However, apart from the few examples we cited, our Lord Jesus fasted for 40 days and nights on an occasion (Matthew 4:2). Other examples of those who incorporated fasting in the Bible include David (11 Samuel 12:16 – 20), Daniel (9:3), John's disciples (Matthew 9:14), Moses (who fasted for 40 days & nights) (Exodus 34:28) and Apostle Paul (Acts 13:1–3) (2 Corinthians 11:27). The Bible highlights the fact that Jesus expected his disciples to fast after his death and resurrection (see Matthew 9:15b). The church at Antioch clearly followed Jesus' teaching. Today's Christians are Jesus' disciples too—so if they choose to fast they will be upholding Jesus' wish.

Partial Fasting

From the examples above, biblical fasting was typically without food and drink. There are however other forms of devotion and prayer that do not wholly fit the definition of fasting denoted by the sense of *covering the mouth*. Partial fasting or what has been dubbed 'Daniel's fast' will fit in this category. Daniel 1:8 –14 and

10:3 presents a situation where Daniel, while eating other foods (not covering the mouth), chose to abstain from *some* types of foods. In the first scenario (1:8 –14), while captive in the foreign land of Babylon, Daniel together with three other Israelites and some local (Babylonian) young men were elected to be specially trained (over 3 years) to work in the Babylonian king's palace. As part of the training, their food was to be provided from the king's palace. Daniel believed that by taking the royal food he would defile himself.[34] The Bible presents Daniel as one who was very devoted to the Jewish religion and worship. He was determined to uphold his worship of Yahweh (God) as prescribed in his religion. There were certain foods that God had declared would religiously defile them if they ate them. Daniel was therefore concerned about defiling himself with the royal food and wine. As a result, he asked not to be served with food from the palace menu during the training period. Instead, he together with his Jewish colleagues resorted to a vegetable based diet in the three year training period. In spite of that, the Jewish boys outperformed the rest of their cohort in appearance, health and every criteria of the training (Daniel 1:1–18). This is a miracle in itself! God's supernatural influence in Daniel and his colleagues' success is evident. There, however, is a question of whether to consider Daniel's action, here, as fasting: (1) the Bible (or Daniel) does not allude to his particular experience as fasting (as he does of his experience in chapter 9:3) and (2) while Daniel chose to abstain from eating the food he considered unclean (defiling), these will be foods he would not ordinarily eat anyway—for religious and cultural reasons. Fasting is however abstaining from eating the food that you would normally eat if you were not fasting—which you will return to eat at the end of the fast.

In the second scenario of chapter 10, Daniel yet again had an occasion where he chose not to eat *some* types of food. He notes, "I ate

---

[34] Carson, A. Donald, France, T. Richard, Motyer J. Alec and Gordon J. Wenham. *"New Bible Commentary."*

no pleasant bread, neither came flesh nor wine in my mouth, neither did I anoint myself at all, till three whole weeks were fulfilled" (Daniel 10:3 AKJV). Here Daniel avoided meat, wine and anointing his body (to make it shine—which was common in his day). He abstained from some food, as well as *oiling* his body—things that he would normally do! This time it was not out of concern to be defiled as in chapter 1. Rather, he was *mourning* (10:2) and *humbling* himself to God (10:12b), after he had received a vision—which foretold a terrible future ahead. To this he says "I had eaten no rich food, no meat or wine had entered my mouth, and I had not anointed myself at all, for the full three weeks" (10:3 NRSV). Although Daniel was eating some foods, and only abstaining from other specific foods (in the three weeks), God responded to him in a phenomenal way. God sent an angel with an answer to his prayer. Many people draw inspiration from and use Daniel's experience here for payers, which involve abstaining from certain foods—as an alternative to whole fasting. Some common examples are: (1) abstaining from meat (where one eats other foods and drinks fluids as normal) and (2) abstaining from all solid food (where one only drinks liquids or in some cases water only)—for specified periods of dedicated prayer. This is what has been widely known as partial fasting.

Fasting in Practice

The Bible does not give specific details of how one ought to fast. As a result, people throughout generations have approached fasting in a variety of ways, based on the broader principles gleaned from the Bible. How people fast is usually determined by what and how they were taught. However, questions of when to fast, how long to fast for and whether to *cover the mouth completely* or to abstain from certain foods (partial fast) can also be influenced by individual need or presenting situation. Sometimes the greater the challenge, the greater the willingness to commit. Also, people on long term treatment of medication that require them to take food will likely choose a form of partial fasting. However, the generally healthy Christians have the opportunity to try different forms of fasting. After trying, people will likely choose a type of fasting that has spiritually impacted them the most, or one they associate with greatest results. Another important aspect that influences how people fast will be the prompting of the Holy Spirit. The Holy Spirit can inspire people to fast, and in some instances specifically direct the form and length of fasting. The bottom line is, however, that through fasting, many have seen greater supernatural (Godly) manifestations and interventions—individually and corporately (as families, groups, churches etc.). I have, over the years, personally experienced the phenomenal experiences of Devine intervention at both levels (personal & corperate), through prayer and fasting. Interestingly, part of this chapter was written while I was in a time of prayer and fasting. Anyway, let me share some life experiences on fasting, to put it into perspective.

Personal Experiences of Prayer and Fasting

Having been raised in a devout Christian family where prayer was held dearly, I had some knowledge of fasting from a young age. It was, however, at the age of 21 that I first became actively involved in prayer fasting on my own accord. Two decades on, fasting has become part of my Christian practice. My fasting is purely that of *'covering the mouth'*. So when I fast; whether I am fasting for part of the day (e.g. from when I wake-up in the morning to 4pm or 6pm) or whole day periods (e.g. 24 – 48hrs), whichever time I choose to dedicate to fast, I do so without food or drink. I am more inclined to the fasting of (*covering the mouth*) where I do not eat and no drink. As a generally healthy individual, I have not had any problems with fasting, health or otherwise. I have on the other hand seen the Lord intervene with phenomenal results in my life and that of many others (I supported with prayers). This includes the healing of cancer, victory over oppressive demonic forces, restoration of troubled relationships, conception problems, opening up of previously unavailable life opportunities etc.

What has reinforced my practice of incorporating fasting in my prayer life is the fact there have been occasions when I have fasted as a result of direct Divine inspiration. I have on occasions received specific Divine inspiration and guidance to pray with fasting for 2 days and 2 nights in order to receive supernatural intervention to difficult situations. On reflection, every time I followed the Spirit's guidance to pray and fast as directed, the difficult situations I was praying over resolved. I can recall two instances that both involved praying and fasting for people who had persistent challenging situations. In both cases, the individuals concerned were troubled by recurrent demonic manifestations—denoting the presence or influence of satanic forces. Having prayed earnestly for the individuals to be free from these situations, the Lord (through the Holy Spirit) specifically guided us to incorporate fasting in our prayers for 2 days and 2 nights. A short time after fasting, the problems were resolved, and the demonic manifestations ceased. It is, however, rare that I have prayed and fasted as a result of having direct instructions or guidance from the Holy Spirit. My prayer and fasting is largely voluntary. I usually fast when I consider that a situation demands more focused and intense prayer. I fast from the time I wake up in the morning, to whatever time I choose at the end of the day. I can do this as a one off, or over a set number of days— where I do not eat and drink throughout the day, until the time I break my fast (usually 4pm or 6pm). There have been occasions and situations that have led me to pray and fast continually for days without eating or drinking. An example is when my brother was battling with 'terminal cancer', which the Lord graciously healed, in response to our prayers (the family and those who supported us).

The Power of Fasting — *Fasting Upholds Other Biblical Principles*

As is the case with spiritual and supernatural issues, it is beyond the human mind to explain in detail how fasting works. Christianity is fundamentally faith-based (John 3:16, Hebrew 11). It is therefore not possible to explain every dimension of it using logic. That is the nature of deity. If we knew every detail of deity, then God would not be God. He would be very limited in sovereignty, and would be equal to humans. However, while we are limited in our understanding of how the supernatural works, we can see the results of our faith and our relationship with God. Nevertheless, fasting is not isolated from other principles taught in the Bible. To appreciate the effect of fasting, we will need to explore some principles of Christian practice that are associated with fasting. In fasting we uphold a number of principles that are already part of Christian faith and required by God. It may be the case that fasting yields divinely inspired results because it incorporates a number of Biblical principles. The Bible generally presents fasting as a form of intense prayer, which equips believers to direct more focus on prayer of petition to God. Directing more focus on God during prayer and fasting allows the spirit to overshadow the negative and evil thoughts. These may include doubt, anxieties and fear—all of which conflict with the more positive qualities that are expected of Christians.

Fasting and Faith

Like prayer, fasting should be a conscious decision. Therefore, taking the step to fast is in itself an act of faith. The decision to pray and fast demonstrates: (1) trust in and dependence on God for answers and guidance and (2) trust in and obedience to God's Word (spoken in the Bible), which demonstrates the need and power of fasting. Why would anyone make the sacrifice and commitment to abstaining from food and or drink if they did not hope or anticipate that God would hear them and respond favorably? The Bible is very clear on how essential faith is. Biblically, faith is "the assurance of things hoped for, the conviction of things not seen" (Hebrews 11:1 NRSV). Faith is highlighted as that key characteristic that believers should possess, which brings about pleasure to God (Hebrews 11:6). Jesus extensively taught His disciples on the importance of faith, and how it is a conduit for accessing Divine intervention in human situations (Matthew 14:30-3; 17:14 –20). Fasting upholds or emphasizes our faith. Fasting is therefore more than just abstaining from food. It fundamentally demonstrates trust in and dependence on God.

Fasting and Humility

Another character that can be attributed to fasting is that of a heart and attitude of humility before God. The writer of the book of Ezra explicitly shows this point. "I proclaimed a fast, **so that we might humble ourselves before our God** and ask him for a safe journey for us and our children, with all our possessions" (Ezra 8:21) (emphasis added). Verse 23 give us the result of their fasting; "So we fasted and petitioned our God about this, and he answered our prayer." The word translated humble in verse 21 in a number of Bible versions has also been translated differently—but however portrays a similar meaning i.e. *'denying ourselves'* (NRSV) or *'afflicting ourselves'* (AKJV). Whichever way we look at it, it denotes a sense of lowliness. It is strongly portrayed in the Bible that the character of *humility* is desirable to God (see 1 Peter 5:5) and moreover strengthens our connection with God. Both James 4:6 and 1 Peter 5:5 in the NIV say "God opposes the proud (those with an arrogant attitude) but shows favor (is kind to or gives grace) to the humble" (brackets added). Many other scriptures uphold and emphasize humility (see Psalms 138:6; Proverbs 11; 12; 29:23;

Mathew 23:12). In 2 Chronicles 7:14 (NASB) God says that, "My people who are called by My name humble themselves and pray and seek My face and turn from their wicked ways, then I will hear from heaven, will forgive their sin and will heal their land". To humble ourselves before God is in itself an act of obedience. Humility, like faith, is an attitude that connects us to the goodness of God, and attracts God's grace—as elaborated in 1 Peter 5:5. Fasting is essentially humbling oneself in order to seek God's grace, attention and intervention (see Isaiah 58:3). By being humble we demonstrate an attitude that is not arrogant towards God or His principles. We moreover express our reliance on God as opposed to self-reliance through humility. Therefore, in being humble we willingly and consciously take a low position (attitude of the heart) to acknowledge that God is greater than us, and that in Him we have hope. This opens the opportunity for God's intervention to flourish.

Also more importantly, humility mitigates the Lord's anger. 2 Chronicles 12 shows how the people of Israel and their king neglected the ways of the Lord. This resulted in their enemies overcoming them, because the Lord God had withdrawn His protection. The King and the leaders however *humbled* themselves before the Lord (12:6). "When the Lord saw that they **humbled themselves**, the word of the Lord came to Shemaiah, saying: "They have **humbled themselves**; I will not destroy them, but I will grant them some deliverance, and my wrath shall not be poured out on Jerusalem by the hand of Shishak" (12:7 ESV) (Emphasis added). From this, we learn that when we humble themselves before God, this can lead to the Lord relenting on the aggravation that we cause Him through disobedience and sin. The Bible strongly shows that fasting is an act of humbling oneself before God. Fasting is therefore much more than a mere act of abstaining from food or drink. Fasting, is at the very least, an act of faith and humbling oneself before God—which can also lead to God overlooking our wrong and withholding the consequence it deserves.

The Occasion of Prayer and Fasting

Time of prayer and fasting is an exciting time and an opportunity for you to tell the Lord everything that is on your heart. Fasting is a choice, and will require self-determination. It starts in the mind. There usually should be a reason or prayer focus that motivates someone to fast. It is helpful to reflect, meditate and focus on your prayer needs before commencing the fast. This will increase the motivation to fast. The devil, however, knows the effect of prayer and fasting, and takes no delight when people fast. It is therefore common to face kinds of discouragement and hindrances when fasting. While these will manifest in the natural, they may be influenced by satanic forces. We do not always know this, as we are not always conscious of everything that occurs in the spiritual sphere. I have, however, known people to develop terrible headaches for example, either the day before commencing the fast or on the very day they start to fast. This is even before their usuall time to eat or drink. Nevertheless, praying and asking the Lord to strengthen you before and during the fast is the most effective mode of overcoming hindrances. This may involve eliciting for prayer support from ministry leaders and other people who understand the principle of fasting. While fasting may seem a challenge, the many people I know who fast regularly do not consider fasting as burdensome as they thought it would be, before they started fasting. Like me, they have come to understand that the benefits of fasting (spiritual discipline and other divinely inspired outcomes of fasting) outweigh the challenge it presents.

Things to Consider When Fasting

As already stated, Christian fasting is not just a matter of abstaining from food and drink. It is about petitioning God through prayer for a specific purpose(s). Therefore, we should be intentional about spending more time in prayer, communicating and expressing our heartfelt desires and needs to the Lord during fasting. Prayer and fasting also present opportunity to combat the power of the devil over one's life, family, ministry etc. through the name of Jesus (Ephesians 6:12, 2 Corinthians 10:4). It is recommended to make time during the course of the day of fasting, to pray asking for forgiveness and cleansing before you make your requests. We learn this from when Daniel fasted in Chapter 9:1–19. It is true that we received forgiveness by being washed by the blood of Jesus when we were born again. It is also true that we struggle with weakness in the flesh, and that there are times when we sin against the Lord. Sin affects our fellowship and communication with God (Isaiah 59: 1–2). Accepting our failures and sin, to God in prayer, is a sign of honoring God and humbling ourselves before Him. This shows that we do not take His grace for granted. It helps clear our minds and conscience from feelings of guilt. It also places us in a better position to approach the Lord in prayer with more confidence and faith (Hebrew 4:16).

We should aim to pray as much as possible during the period of prayer and fasting. This may include finding a place where you can be alone, and pray to Jesus (Philippians 4:6). Others find it helpful to disengage from regular activities e.g. to take time off work to have time of prayer and meditation without disturbances, for the entire period of prayer and fasting. Like many others, I have found taking time to go away to a place where there is not much activity e.g. a retreat centre or hotel room very beneficial. Of course this is not always possible. Nevertheless, one can pray quietly in their heart when around other people e.g. at work, college etc., but should also allow for time to freely express oneself alone to the Lord in prayer, in an unrestricted place. At the end of the set prayer period, it is encouraged not to eat food or drink before praying. The closing prayer is used to thank the Lord for the strength to fast, as well as to mark the end of the fast. It is also uplifting for people to make the closing prayer together when fasting as a group. If people cannot meet physically, they can agree a time to pray, each person in their own location. People have today adopted other means of praying together remotely through skype and conference calls etc.

Apart from confession, a time of prayer and fasting is also a time to be more conscious of and intentional about avoiding sin, overcoming temptation and doing good. Of course this is what Christians should do all the time! We, however, know that there are times in life when we drop our guard on these principles, as we get embroiled in the demands of day to day life. The time of fasting is nonetheless dedicated to connecting with God more intensely. It is, therefore, reasonable to consider that such a time of consecration will demand more thought and seriousness about how we conduct ourselves. In Isaiah 58:3-4, God indicates that the effectiveness of fasting, in part, depends on how we conduct themselves during the time of fasting. The NLT Bible gives more clarity on this; "We have fasted before you!' they say. 'Why aren't you impressed? We have been very hard on ourselves, and you don't even notice it!' "I will tell you why!" I respond. "It's because you are fasting to please yourselves. Even while you fast, you keep oppressing your workers. What good is fasting when you keep on fighting and quarreling? This kind of fasting will never get you anywhere with me." It is not to say that it is ok to do wrong things when not fasting. Isaiah 58 is clear that the lifestyle of God's people should constantly be in line with God. In fact, the chapter shows that we are expected to live Godly lives even outside of fasting. The point is, however, that there is more expectation to demonstrate a life that is consistent with the Word of God when fasting. This makes fasting more meaningful and effective (see whole chapter of Isiah 58).

Apart from prayer, or rather to support prayer, reading the Bible is a very effective means of maintaining focus on God when fasting. This aids us to remain focused on the principles of God's Word. Because the temptation of focusing on other things in life during fasting is real, reading the Bible more while fasting has various benefits. Firstly, reading the Bible at any time is one of the most powerful ways we can connect with God and access His Power. Secondly, there are many benefits associated with reading the Bible, particularly when fasting (see Romans 10:17; Hebrews 4:12; 2 Timothy 3:16; Psalms 119:11; Job 23:12). In addition to Bible reading, I have found playing and listening to Christian music emotionally and spiritually stimulating. It facilitates for the mind to remain focused on the Lord.

Conclusion

Fasting is a very spiritually stimulating form of prayer that is associated with faith-building, humbling ourselves before God, which attracts God's grace for the forgiveness and absolving of the consequences that our continuing sin deserves. From Bible times to present day Christianity, the results of fasting are evident. While it may be perceived as a burden, fasting can be very exciting. Like every Christian practice, fasting is not to be obligatory. It is a personal decision. It can be more stimulating to fast as a group e.g. as a couple, family, group of friends or collectively as a church. Even then, it should be done in agreement. In our church we have a number of occasions where we pray and fast for various purposes, and for different periods. One of the most anticipated prayer and fasting occasions is the 2 day (and night) weekend fasting that we hold once a year. Over the years, we have seen phenomenal outpourings of the Holy Spirit and the manifestation of God's working. Many people's prayer lives and resilience have been impacted through this prayer. Year after year, we see a significant proportion of our members opting to participate in this life-changing activity. It is a time where we spend most of the weekend at church with various meetings, to worship, which gives us the opportunity to learn from the Bible, and to pray and petition the Lord over individual and collective petitions. The meetings run from Friday night, through Saturday, ending on Sunday morning where we break the fast, and eat and drink.

Disclaimer

The insights of fasting presented in this book draw from: (1) Biblical experiences and teachings of fasting, (2) Christian principles that are associated with fasting and (3) real life experiences of contemporary fasting (personal experiences and that of others). It is not a prescriptive resource. I therefore entreat readers who are seeking to explore the practice of fasting to consider their own situation, and make their own judgement on the nature and period of fasting they wish to follow. Those with medical conditions and those taking regular medication, which may be affected by not eating or drinking, should consult their doctor for advice if they consider to fast.

CHAPTER 13

Epilogue

I have covered a number of areas that are associated with facing life challenges and difficulties in this book. I have highlighted the fact that we are inhabitants of a fallen world, which was defiled by disobedience and sin. Consequently, life throws unpleasant experiences that negatively impact our enjoyment of it. We cannot escape from this reality. It is a reality that is clearly highlighted in the Word of God. Some of these experiences can be intense and may be long lasting. As elaborated in earlier chapters, there are various factors that influence our experience of these situations. In some circumstances, people contribute to situations that affect them. This means that some of the hardships we face in life are caused by our own making, and that of others around us. It is clear that from the beginning, Adam and Eve suffered the consequences of their actions when they disobeyed God. Our good Lord however forgives our sin and wrong doing when we ask Him. This does not take away the fact that many of our life choices and actions produce consequences. Life decisions and choices are very crucial at every stage of our lives. If I had a second chance to live my life over again I would definitely change a good number of decisions and choices I made in the past. I am very sure that this applies to many of us. As already discussed, we should not dwell on the mistakes of life. On the contrary, we should make the most of the present life and that which is ahead, in Christ Jesus.

I have also expounded on the fact that some difficult situations we face are caused by supernatural factors— some by Satan's activity, and still others are allowed by God for some special purpose. It may be difficult to always know the driving force behind your situation. What you should however know is that whatever the cause, Jesus loves you, and is able to deliver you from all situations. Cast all your burdens on Him and trust that He will sustain you (Psalm 55:22; 1 Peter 5:7). After we have surrendered our situations to Him, we should trust that He has the power to remove the burden, and to give us strength to endure in time of challenges. It should however be accepted that healing and restoration can be a process. Some situations will take time to resolve. It demands patience and continually trusting in the Lord.

The Right Attitude

I am confident that many will find the insights I share in this book helpful and relevant to their situation. I, on the other hand, accept that there may be some who will find themselves in the same situation even after exploring and applying the insights and principles I share in this book. If that applies to someone who has read this book, I would encourage them, in the way that I normally encourage myself using the '4 I will statements':

1. I will continue to love and have faith in my Lord in spite of my situation.
2. I will do my best to live a prayerful life and try by all means to live peaceably with everyone.
3. I will continue to exercise my God-given authority in Christ to denounce satanic activities in my life.
4. I will continue to serve the Lord.

After having followed all the principles highlighted in this book, and embraced the *4 I will-statements*—I will consider that whatever comes my way is God's will. I will take the situation to be one of the situations which I do not need to do anything about. Coming to this state of understanding is not easy. It is however something that can be worked towards. If achieved, it takes away anxieties caused by the situation and provides peace and comfort in the face of a challenge.

Do Not Suffer in Isolation

In closing, the focus of this book is concerned with empowering the believer to self-explore how to understand and respond to life situations, using biblical principles. I, however, acknowledge that there may be occasions when it will be more challenging to face difficult life situations without the help of others. Christian counselling and prayer support from others are effective forms of support that are in-line with the teaching of the Bible. Believers should not struggle on their own and become overwhelmed by life difficulties in isolation. The Lord has equipped the church with people who are able to support others, pastorally. Pastors and those with pastoral responsibility and calling are a valuable source of support that God has provided to the body of believers. Counselling generally employs talking therapy. It offers people the opportunity to open up about their challenges and feelings to a trained and trusted minister and or professional, who is able to listen to them in confidence. The counsellor will support the individual to explore and to manage negative thoughts or feelings. Christian/ Biblical counselling will work in a similar way, and will be based on biblical (God inspired) principles. Through the influence of the Holy Spirit, the individual receiving counselling will be restored back to the realization that in God, they are actually stronger than what they may feel. This will help them to cope with challenges, find solutions to their problems or look at their situation differently (more positively). They will experience spiritual renewal—which is a foundation of living a life of peace and comfort.

I hope that I have been able to provide the readers with a framework that will help them explore and respond to their own situations and those of others based on biblical insights. Let us continue to trust the Lord to resolve our situations, in order to experience peace and maintain a flourishing relationship with Him— even in the midst of life challenges.

If you find this resource useful, please stay connected through the book website and blog:

www.lightingupthedark-tunnelmoments.com